# TOOL TALES

# TOOL TALES

*Stories and Tips for the Antique Tool Collector*

HERBERT P. KEAN

*Astragal Press*　　*Mendham, New Jersey*

*Published by*

The Astragal Press
P.O. Box 239
Mendham, NJ 07945-0239

Copyright 2002 by Herbert P. Kean

All rights reserved. No part of this book may be reproduced or transmitted in any form or by any means, electrical or mechanical, including photocopying, recording, or by any information or retrieval system, without the written permission of the Publisher, except where permitted by law.

*Cover Design by*: Donald Kahn
*Cover Sketch by*: Larry Fuhro
*Photographs by*: Robert Garay
*Cartoons by*: Harry O'Neill
*Sketches by*: Herbert P. Kean

Library of Congress Control Number 2002107406
ISBN 1-931626-05-7

*Printed in the United States of America*

# TABLE OF CONTENTS

# INTRODUCTION

For almost 25 years I have been writing short articles about antique tools. Some were merely stories, while others were informational or how-to-do treatises. They were mostly written for *The Tool Shed*, the periodical for the Collectors of Rare And Familiar Tools Society (CRAFTS) of New Jersey tool club. But others were published in *The New Book of Knowledge* encyclopedia; *Carpenter* magazine, from the United Brotherhood of Carpenters & Joiners of America; *Chip Chats* magazine, from the National Wood Carvers Association; *The Chronicle*, from the Early American Industries Association; and *Patinagram*, from the Potomac Antique Tools and Industries Association. In all I wrote over 100 articles for these organizations as well as many other museums, libraries and newspapers. The 50 that are reprinted here are a sampling of the ones that I consider the best.

Many of the stories have a bit of humor running through them. Some are more technical presentations. A few are accounts of trips taken by myself and my wife, Doris, including a lot of fond memories and nostalgia. But all have as their basic theme: ANTIQUE TOOLS.

The cartoons (except the "exploding window" one, done by my wife) were created by the late Harry O'Neill, our Vice President in the early days of CRAFTS. The photography was done by Bob Garay, our current *Tool Shed* editor.

The year each article was written is under the title. They are not in chronological order. So watch out for references to prices or times (such as "years ago"), etc. You will have to correlate them with the year written.

I am still writing and giving presentations. It is a super hobby in addition to collecting. It's nice to know that some of these stories and articles got a chuckle from the original readers. Some gave new information. Hopefully this compilation will entertain and inform you as well.

# 1

## THE BEGINNING (2001)

One of the most frequent questions asked of anyone who makes a hobby presentation is, "How did you get started in that field?" I get that one all the time. It's a legitimate question, and when it's directed at a "storyteller," the answer is usually an interesting one. Here is mine.

A few years before the 1976 Bicentennial my wife Doris was assisting an interior decorator (now called interior designer) in redoing the office of an executive of a large corporation. He was known to be a "man's man," and he mentioned that he would like to have his office reflect that. Doris and her friend weren't sure what that meant, so they asked me. I felt that it had to do with the individual, but on a general basis it would mean that the fellow liked sports, hunting, fishing, horseback riding, etc.

So they asked the executive if he wanted guns, deer heads, fishing equipment or the likes adorning the walls. He didn't hunt, fish or ride, nor was he deeply interested in any given sport. No help there. But he stated that whatever they chose to do would probably be OK, as long as they advised him first.

They needed small furniture, pictures, and accessories in addition to the "manly objects," so they made an appointment with one of their dealers. I was asked to come along as the sherpa porter to lug all the stuff back. I had been on those forages before and they were awfully boring. I usually fell asleep in the wagon waiting for them to finish their buying.

This time I brought along a book to read, but never got very far into it before I fell asleep. I was rudely awakened by the girls tugging at my arm in a very excited manner. "We found the manly stuff," they kept saying over and over. In somewhat of a daze I was lead into the shop where the owner was all smiles and welcoming me profusely. (He never thought much of me before, as I usually turned my nose up at his "lovely things.")

He took me to the back of the shop and gingerly took a cloth off a pile of unbelievable junk. Almost everything was rusted or falling apart. He was able to force a smile as he told me how "utterly perfect these things would be for the job. And they would be free for the taking!" His basic purpose was to get them out of his shop as quickly and as quietly as possible. They were originally brought in by his helper as part of an estate buy. The helper, a local lad, never realized how offensive this "pile of junk" was to his sophisticated New Yorker boss.

I took Doris aside and told her that if taking this junk would make a better deal for the other stuff she was buying, I would load it into the wagon last, and drop it off at the dump on the way home. Everyone was happy.

However, it rained on the way home, and I decided to dump the junk the next day. But that night I was overcome by curiosity. I took a few pieces from the wagon into the basement to try to make head or tail out of what they did. It was fairly obvious that they were tools or implements of some kind, but their functions were still a question. I had to put some of the parts together like a jig-saw puzzle. But slowly the answers came. They were very old carpenter tools, in such a state of disrepair that they were almost unrecognizable.

I cleaned up an old wooden brace with brass sides which were previously black with oxidation. It really didn't look that bad. Pretty enough to satisfy the girls, and gutsy enough to be considered manly. Maybe that wacko dealer was not so far off after all. I quickly took it up to Doris, who proclaimed in utter amazement that, "The finish looks like good furniture, and it could easily be considered a *handsome* piece." She had to immediately phone her friend to tell her that the decoration problem was solved. Just a call to the exec for approval was all that was needed. Woe unto me, I had just hoisted myself on my own petard. I would now have to clean and fix all these "manly" pieces.

"Yes, yes, old tools would be terrific conversation pieces, but someone would have to explain what they were," was the approval response. I was getting deeper and deeper into this thing, and curiously not minding it as much as I let on. The only two references available were Eric Sloane's book *A Museum of Early American Tools* and Henry Mercer's book *Ancient Carpenters' Tools*. But they were enough to do the job, as the ones not in the book I kept for myself.

The evenings during the next week were exciting for me, as one by one I got those old relics to work and look like something. Doris kept bringing me cool drinks in the basement, as she realized that she had to keep my spirits up. (I did an enormous amount of complaining.) I put the smaller pieces on barn boards, and made narrow shelves for the larger ones. Naturally, I was the one who had to mount them in the office.

When the Monday morning came, after the weekend of redecorating, the executive was enthralled with the tools. The girls were a little disappointed that he didn't look at all their other work first. But all-in-all it was a huge success.

The leftovers formed my new hobby. I started with a dozen or so antique tools and never looked back. That day, in that shop, was a true red letter event in my life, and it became the starting point for this book.

# 2

## NO TOOLING TODAY
## (1986)

Some summers ago, Doris and I decided to take a Sunday ride to the Catskills — just for the scenery. When we are out for a ride, and not antiquing, the "rule" is that only once or twice during the day am I allowed an antique stop. I was feeling guilty about the fiasco of a ride we had the week before, so I benevolently announced that there would be "no tooling today." The look of disbelief I got was based upon instant replays of years of similar announcements.

I was a prince of a person all morning, but at lunch we stopped at a restaurant that had tools hanging on the walls. I had long since refrained from sneering at these touristy tools, because I once found an Aaron Smith complex molder in just such a place. The owner and I talked a bit while waiting for the meal, and I found out that he bought most of his collection from an antique dealer "up in the woods." He graciously gave me directions (once I was sure Doris was out of earshot).

Now I'm not the world's best on directions, particularly when the other guy is all screwed-up also. So when I got lost trying to pull off the let's-try-this-back-road-for-the-terrific-scenery trick, I had to admit that my no-tooling promise would have to be scrapped on the pile of good intentions.

She was delighted to get in one of her famous "I knew you couldn't do it!" remarks. It seemed like a fair exchange.

However, after two wrong farmhouses and a kid on a bike, we finally found the dealer. He wasn't in the woods, but in the sticks — the type of area Doris calls "ticky-tacky," and is filled with junk cars, falling-down barns, and old appliances on the front porches. But, he did have a quonset hut with a sign reading ANTIQUES. I mentioned that it didn't appear as if he had much of interest, and I'd only be a few minutes. Besides, as late as it now was, we could start right back and have a nice leisurely dinner at one of our favorite country inns.

It was miserably hot that day, and Doris decided to come into the hut rather than wait in the car. The hut held an unusual array of saleable items that surprised both of us, but unfortunately the meager number of tools were all of the farm type. We picked out some nice things, and as we were paying the fellow, I asked the stereotyped question (more out of habit than reason), "Do you have any other tools somewhere else?"

He took us to a rusty 20-foot truck trailer attached to the back of the hut. When he opened the trailer door, all I can remember is the Red Sea opening up to a full display of Fourth of July fireworks! The whole trailer was loaded, and I mean loaded, with tools. He explained that he got these tools sometime back but had no room in the hut, so he bought the trailer just for them. "Trouble is I haven't put up a sign yet, and I keep forgetting to mention them," he apologized. It seemed to me that he really wanted to hold onto them for a while, but even though nothing was priced, he did say *everything* was for sale. The parallel about the kid in the candy shop couldn't come close to matching this situation.

Most of the tools were routine, but I could see snatches of greatness here and there, and I knew it was going to take some digging. Doris completely gave up at this point, went back to the car, turned on the air conditioning, and curled up with her Sunday *New York Times* — which she always brings along for such emergencies.

There was some semblance of order to the piles and shelves. All augers were in one spot, and axes and saws were in others. Planes were scattered, but the metal planes were all on two racks of shelves. It was the first time I ever saw Stanley planes complete— all depth stops, cutters, etc. Boxes of blades were with each piece, not always the right box, but everything matched up in the end.

It didn't take long before the blast-furnace temperature in that trailer had me wringing wet. It's amazing how physical discomforts can disappear when the adrenaline is flowing. I was an absolute mess of sweat and dirt, but grinning like a banshee.

I found an entire set of Japanese tools, which I had never seen before, and I became intrigued with figuring them out. She-who-must-be-obeyed started complaining about the late hour, and as the station wagon was going to be filled anyway, I left the Japanese stuff behind. Also left behind were hundreds of common planes that I didn't take out into the light to check for signatures. Eighteenth-century planes were not that popular then.

But my keepers were loaded as fast as I could get them through his "checkout." This consisted of pricing by armfuls, but with some lapses of logic. For example, a #45 was the same price as a #41. Beech plows and boxwood plows were equal — but braces with brass on them were more expensive than the all wood ones. I also had to buy some pieces that he was "pushing," such as four crummy hand saws. We made a date for a return trip, and the Catskills became one of my favorite rides.

Most of the tools taken from this trailer were cleaned up and sold to the original members of CRAFTS, way back in the days of the Saturday Sales in Chatham. The rest are in my collection and still stir fond memories of that exciting day.

P.S. With me looking like a coal miner and the car loaded to the roof rack, Doris and I never made it to the fancy inn for dinner. One more broken promise created by the lure of antique tools.

# 3

## GOOSEWING AXES
## (1985)

*Tool Shed Editor's Note: The following is a slightly revised version of an article that first appeared in The Tool Shed in September, 1979. Nothing in these pages, before or since, stirred so much interest. Even today, more than five years later, we receive requests for copies — two arrived just before Christmas. Because the article continues to draw attention, we thought that it would be appropriate to reprint it.*

The goosewing is one of the most celebrated of all the edge cutting tools. According to Eric Sloane, it once competed in an art contest! Although indicators exist that it might have been used as a medieval fighting axe, it is a functional broad axe used basically for hewing.

Various shapes have their origins in different countries and are known as turkey wings, angel wings, etc. The earliest shape shown in Mercer's *Ancient Carpenters' Tools* is the Central European style of the 16th century. See Fig. 1. The bulk of the American axes were made in Pennsylvania from the 18th to the mid-19th centuries. See Fig. 2. However, foreign axes have been made well into the 20th century. German troop trucks carried goosewings as utility side axes during World War II. Some axes are still made in Scandinavia and Spain, and reproductions are coming out of Austria even today.

**Fig. 1. Right-Handed**

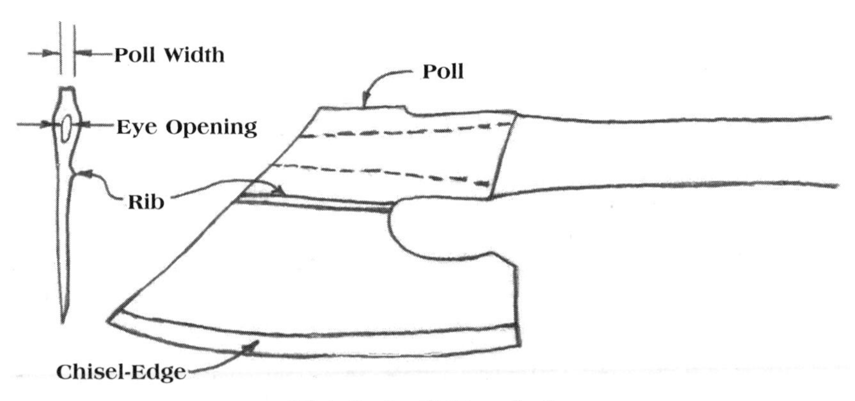


**Fig. 2. Left-Handed**

The skill required in forging a goosewing far exceeds that needed for the common broad axe. Instead of a single roll-around and lap with a laid-in piece of steel, the goosewing requires four separate pieces. Kauffman, in *American Axes*, gives an excellent description of this technique; and although there may have been other ways, his analysis is certainly a logical alternative. Axes made by lesser blacksmiths clearly show the voids and seams of this construction.

The use of the goosewing is not as speculative as its history. Hewing was its main purpose. Weighing up to nine pounds, and with its 13" (average) handle, it is obvious that the axe was not swung as a felling axe. It is powered diagonally downward with a short stroke with the outside hand, and guided for proper angle with the inside hand. The center of balance almost allows a one-handed swing. The experienced hewer lets the heavier axes cut under their own weight.

The axe being asymmetrical, the smith had to forge both right-handed and left-handed styles. A right-handed goosewing is designed to be used on the right side of the log with your right hand forward. It is not always for a right-handed person! Many right-handed people get better accuracy by *guiding* with their right hand. As hewing demands considerable accuracy, some right-handed hewers use left-handed axes and work from the left side.

The predominant reason for right and left-handed axes, however, was for working the grain "up" or "down" similar to double beaders and double routers. Not every hewer had a *pair* of goosewings, as there were 44 right-handed and only 26 left-handed axes tallied in this study. For those people using only one axe, it is obvious that right-handed axes were preferred.

The more common argument today is the origin of the axe. Those Pennsylvania makers who signed their axes left no doubt as to origin, and help us today to compare the unsigned axes. No rule is without exception, and unsigned axes should be judged by the *total number* of indicating characteristics.

Twenty-four of the 70 axes were studied closely and 28 separate characteristics were recorded for each axe. Only seven characteristics showed any correlating significance between American and foreign origin, and they are listed below:

1. Axes with narrow eye openings on the forward end (under 3/8") are almost always American.

2. Highly decorated pieces are more Germanic.

3. Most Europeans swayed their handles; Americans usually forged more cant in the eye and used a straighter handle.

4. Grainy, pocked or rough "charcoal" iron is more American than the smoother, higher quality iron of Europe.

5. European axes usually have higher ribs; many American axes have no ribs at all.

6. Polls wider than 3/4" are predominantly European.

Some of the known Pennsylvania makers were: Addams, Stohler, Stahler, His, Sener, Rohrbach, and Beatty (rare). The only New Jersey maker found was Luke Miller (ca. 1780) of Madison. New York boasts of L. & I. J. White.

It must be remembered that many of the American axe makers got their skills in their mother countries, predominantly Germany, and copied some or all of the European characteristics when first arriving in this country. These early axes are hard to categorize. The quality of the iron is their most pertinent characteristic.

The goosewing is generally the focal point of a display or collection, and rightly so. With its graceful and dramatic form, it represents both strength and finesse, a rare combination.

(Thanks to my friends in Pennsylvania for their help and advice: Frank Kerr, Dallas John, Merk Beitler, and Ben Alexander.)

# 4

## SPEAKING THE LANGUAGE
## (1980)

Although the Space Program engineers will forever hold the record for confounding our language, we antiquers come close when it comes to saying things that really have different meanings. Perhaps it is the politeness of our breed. Below are ten such sayings you may recognize — from either the buying or the selling end.

1. "Mmmm, it is an *interesting* piece." Real meaning: My god, is it ugly!

2. "I can't come down any further, that's what I paid for it." Real meaning: Take it or leave it, you're starting to bug me.

3. "This is a very early piece." Real meaning: It was bought at Englishtown at 4 o'clock in the morning.

4. "They are a set." Real meaning: They came to the sale in the same box.

5. "It's a shame you didn't come by this morning, I had all kinds of good tools." Real meaning: I had one jackplane (no wedge), one rusty drawknife and two monkey wrenches.

6. "I know it doesn't have a lever cap, that's why my price is so low." Real meaning: What's a lever cap?

7. "Oh, I heard about that sale, but I'm not going. Everything is too high." Real meaning: I hope he forgets about it, so I don't bump into him there.

8. "Sure it looks rough, but I bought it for parts only." Real meaning: How could I have made such a mistake?

9. "You'll never believe what I paid for it." Real meaning: Eat your heart out!

10. "Maybe I did think it was ebony, but it's still better than putting money in the bank." Real meaning: If I don't get these woods right, I'm going to kill myself!

**He gave a sort of conditional answer to my offer. He said: "When Hell freezes over!"**

# 5

## THE STANLEY #1 FAKE
## (1980)

If you look at a fake Stanley #1 next to an authentic one, it is hard to believe that anyone would not detect the fake. But by itself on an auction block, or under the excitement of a bargain, it is possible that the fake could pass, which is exactly what the perpetrator depended on.

The defects, errors and sloppy workmanship involved were allowed only to the extent that they did not severely detract from the overall impression. To this degree the duplicator kept smoothing down the roughly cast parts until they were passable. The fact that they were made considerably undersized by doing this did not bother him. Who would think of measuring? Who would be carrying Sellens' book *The Stanley Plane* at that precise moment anyway?

So today there are a goodly number of these fakes floating around, and more will possibly show up as owners realize what they have purchased. Listed below are the incongruities that I picked up from one plane graciously loaned to me by Lee Murray, who has been instrumental in circulating warnings about the spurious #1's.

Body: Overall length to rear of handle extension is only 5½ inches (approximately ¼ inches short). Also, the handle extension is flat with the sole instead of being upraised approximately 1/32 inches. See Fig. 1.

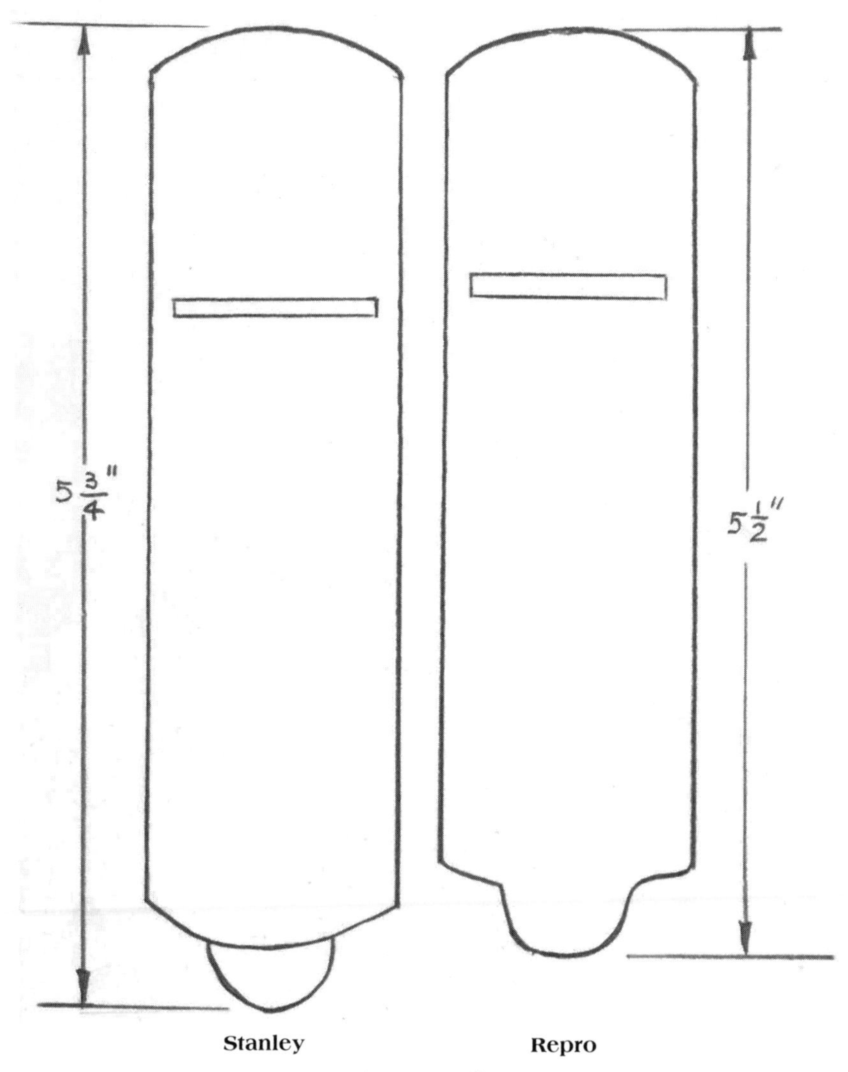


**Fig. 1. Sole**

Knob & Handle Studs: wrong thread pitch.

Knob: Too small; and made of two pieces. See Fig. 2.

Handle: Too short. See Fig. 3

Knob & Handle Nuts: Poorly machined, with hacksawed slots; wrong thread pitch. Handle nut too short (prevents tightening).

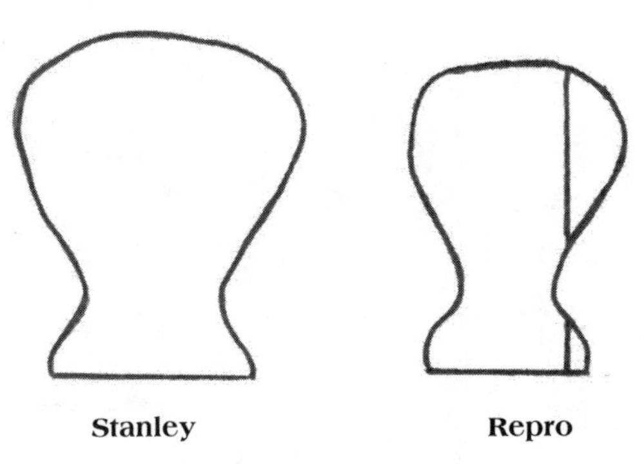

Stanley Repro

Fig. 2. Knob

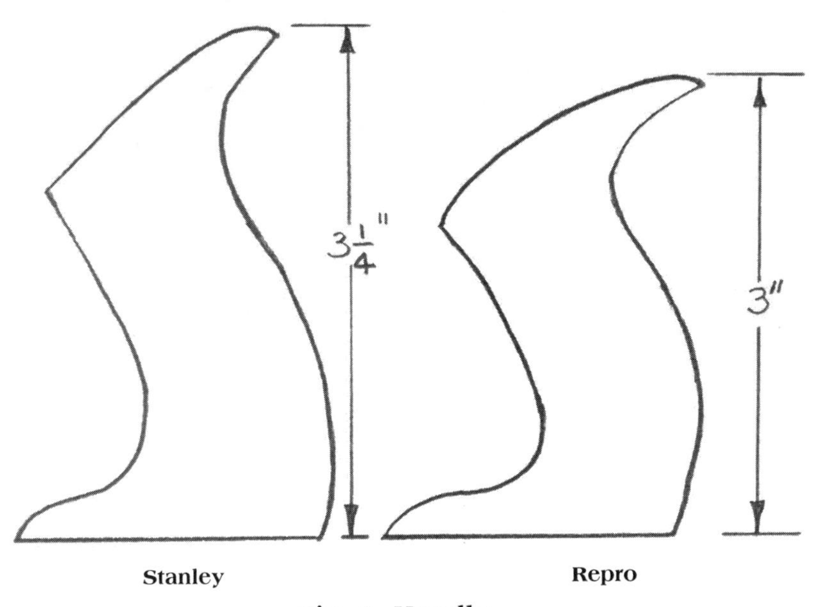


Stanley Repro

Fig. 3. Handle

Lever Cap: Too small all around, and porous. Rivet is brass instead of steel. Lever slot is far too deep. See Fig. 4.

Cap Iron: Tang hole filed instead of punched. Tension radius is too small and is non-functional. See Fig. 5.

Connecting Screw: Raggedly machined and doesn't fit through mating hole in the cutting iron.

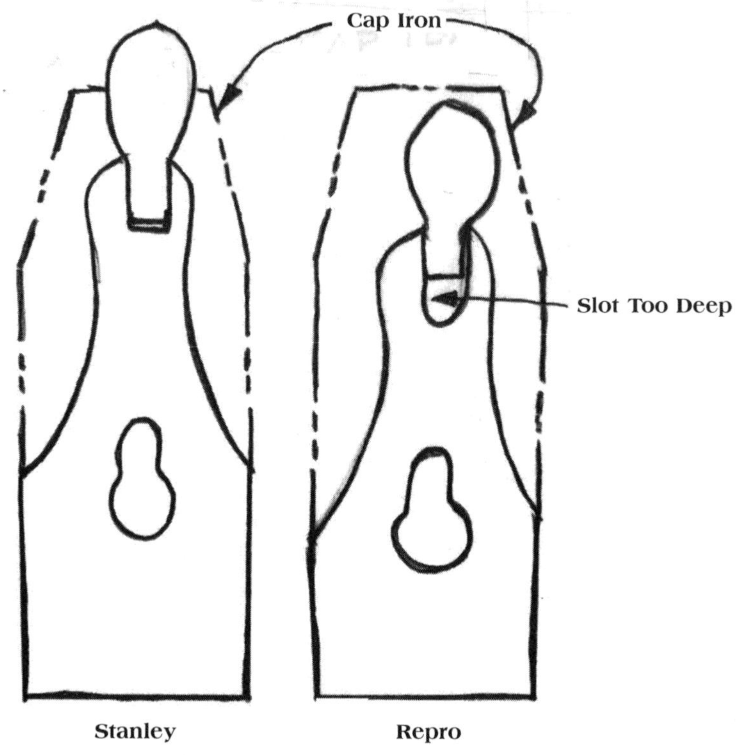


**Fig. 4. Lever Cap**

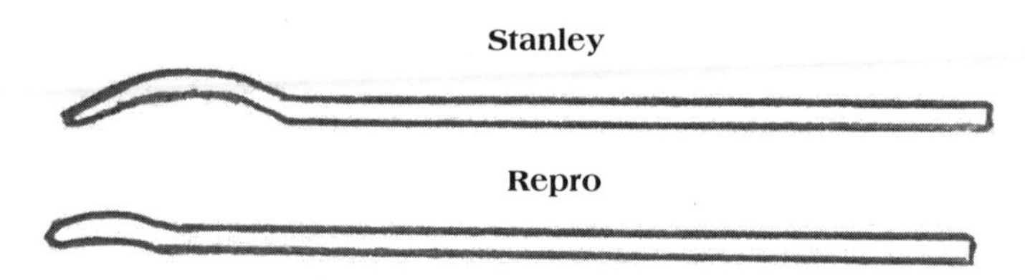


**Fig. 5. Cap Iron (Side View)**

Cutting Iron: stamping out-of-square and letters are not all correct size. See Fig. 6.

Frog: Outline very rough and sanded fully on sides.

Frog Screws: Standard round-head instead of Stanley round-head.

Frog Washers: Missing.

**Fig. 6. Marking on Iron**

Lever Cap Screw: Standard round-head instead of Stanley oval-head.

Adjustment Knob: Heavy porosity. No sign of finishing except with file.

Adjustment Knob Stud: Diameter and thread pitch wrong.

Weight: 7/8 lb. instead of 1 1/8 lb.

Based upon the markings, the reverse key slot in the cutting iron, and the right-hand thread in the adjustment knob stud, my guess is that it was copied from a true #1 of the 1880 vintage. I feel that it was directly cast and smoothed undersize. The "just-get-by" attitude and the "for-profit" motivation rules out the making of patterns. Also, the direct casting (and its resultant shrinkage). would account for part of the undersize conditions.

Hopefully the information given above will help in preventing any further sales of these fakes.

# 6

## CRAFTS — A GENESIS
### (1987)

I doubt that the expression "Thank God It's Friday" ever started with a married man. There were times when I would just as soon skip Saturday altogether, as it was *chore day*. Fix the shutters, cement the crack in the basement, rake the leaves, cut the lawn — all of the necessities of suburban living.

But some of us figured a way out of this dilemma. My particular technique stemmed from my prior training in getting out for the Friday night poker games. It was all in the presentation! If you were merely going to a poker game to drink beer, eat bologna sandwiches, and tell lies, it wouldn't sell. You had to present something that had pizazz, like the Bi-Weekly Fathers Club or the West Side Civic Organization. Now you had a weapon. How could anyone prevent you from attending such a necessary function as these grand titles alluded to?

Well, CRAFTS was born in this creative atmosphere. Five guys were sitting together at a Pennsylvania auction, slapping their knees at the stories they had to tell to get away that day. One of the geniuses proposed a plan to continue the evasive action under the guise of a club (you could almost taste the bologna sandwiches).

During this period, I had my own plan for Saturdays. I sold tools all day. The idea about the "Club" was introduced during one of my Saturday Sales and was immediately welcomed by every man in the room.

Ed Bragg, one of the "doers" in the crowd, volunteered to start it off. No one thought he was really going to do it — just whip out a letter or two to prove that we had an important place to go on Saturdays.

But Ed called us together for our first Charter Member Executive Directors Meeting (you couldn't beat that for class). It was a shocker when he gave us all copies of a proposed charter, etc. We were so dumbfounded that we never realized that meeting day was *Sunday*, and only five times per year.

To this day I think Ed was a double-agent and was well paid off by the Wives Club. How else did he get all that money to buy his mansion in up-state New York, and why did he move away so quickly?

So there we were — leaderless, meeting on the wrong day, and still raking leaves. It wasn't a pretty sight.

Steve Zluky was the only one among us who didn't complain. It seemed that his background dictated hard work and no crying. Perfect for President! We convinced him to make the sacrifice for the good of "mankind." We also made all kinds of promises about the help he would get.

I'm proud to say that the "dirty dozen" (there were twelve of us by then) came through. And why not? If we had a legitimate Club that collected legitimate things, then we could go to legitimate Saturday auctions. How sweet it was.

We even started an auction of our own. This required many Saturdays of preparation, and of course the big event itself was on a Saturday. We were on a roll. It was now necessary to attend auctions in far-away places, with hotel room bull-sessions and the whole bit. Good club members participate, don't they?

I don't know where we lost control but little by little, people started writing books and getting serious. The Executive Directors Meeting became an actual meeting, and the auctions became work. It looked like we had gone full circle.

We now call upon our leaders to bring us back to the Promised Land — back to the hidden Saturdays. Tools are nice, but they have taken over our lives. Let's get back to the fun days — the days of the tall stories and the bologna sandwiches.

How about some of you younger fellows stepping up and letting us old-timers just "fade away"? (We'll make it worth your while.)

NEW JERSEY TOOL COLLECTORS ORGANIZE

# 7

## FUNCTION AND APPEARANCE FIRST (1983)

*This article was published in the EAIA Chronicle.*

For many years, I've read articles from the purists about what not to do when restoring tools. The trouble is that there have been relatively few expressions from the collectors who are more realistic about restoration. As I sat down to take up the pen for the latter group, I felt a slight apprehension. It was almost as if I would be challenging motherhood or the flag. I could end up being "drummed out of the corps" or "tarred and feathered" or, even worse, have all my wire wheels confiscated in the dead of the night. So, in defense, I have organized the Legion of Realists. Our motto is: Function and Appearance First.

I would like to list a few of the "don'ts" compiled from various members of our counterparts, the Purists:

Don't use wire wheels.
Don't use strippers.
Don't use stains.
Don't use emery paper.
Don't use sandpaper.
Don't use paint or polish.
Don't use linseed oil.
Don't use repro parts.

There are very few things that they will grant permission to use. And why? Their arguments are:

1) Philosophically — future historians will be confused.

2) Morally — the integrity of the piece will be destroyed.

3) Aesthetically — the patina will be lost.

The Legion would like to reply to these conjectures.

1) Historians will always be confused if they don't dig into the realistic nature of life rather than the surface evidence. Man has always preserved and restored artifacts, and for the most part, has always been able to distinguish the restoration from the original. An interesting technique, proposed by one of Vermont's finest restorers, is to identify replaced pieces on the underside. However, fakes for profit will continue to be produced by unscrupulous people. We are best protected by learning the facts necessary to detect good from bad. A perfect example of this is the now famous Stanley #1 fraud. It was only after the publication of warnings and detailed descriptions that the market dried up for these fakes. I am proud to say that this author wrote one of the earliest descriptive exposes on these fakes. (Sept. 1980, CRAFTS, *Tool Shed*).

In contrast to the Stanley #1 fiasco, there is a Brooklyn cabinetmaker who produces magnificent tools that are not only breathtaking, but far enough out of accord with antique styling that they are only momentarily confused with antiques. He has never represented them as anything but contemporary. Where is it written that he cannot continue this great pleasure? It is as much a part of our present society to go back to handcraft as it was a necessity to do so 200 years ago. Let the historians record this era as such — a need to break away from computerized production lines and shoddy products. The repros of our great artisans show a desire to return to prideful workmanship. And like all things good, if they fall into deceiving hands, we must accept that as a risk of their being.

2) Integrity is not destroyed by surface changes, repairs, replacements, etc. If they are poorly done, they will reflect exactly that — a sloppy job. If they are well done, with correct materials (whether recent or yesteryear), they will

demonstrate the resiliency of the design to stand up under periodic maintenance. Are we any less of a person after a haircut? If we must have dentures to function, has our integrity been destroyed? Wouldn't you rather have a complete tool, correct in function and appearance, than one in such a disheveled state that it is hard to determine its purpose? The Legion of Realists answer resoundingly, YES !

3) Patina is generally taken to mean the tone of a material brought on by time and useage. Rust is an abusive form of patina. No one likes rust. No craftsman would allow it. Very few prideful craftsmen will even allow the discoloration that precedes rust. So then why is this discoloration held sacred by the purists? To the realist, it seems correct on a hand-forged traveler but out of place on the working surface of a Stanley plane. The highlighted effect of worn handles are natural to any tool and quite good looking, but filth is unnatural to the working life of the tool and should be removed.

The cry for not removing these unpleasant obstructions with wire wheels and strippers is that "you will lose the patina." There are wire wheels fine enough that, when run at lower speeds (1,725 RPM or less), will not even abrade your skin; strippers that when applied with #4/0 steel wool and rubbed immediately, take only infinitesimal amounts of surface film. Naturally, some of the original finish will be removed if you wish to eliminate the deep crud, but the nice part is that the old look can be returned. The external character of wood is much deeper than you think. Aniline stains can match the original color as close as the eye can perceive, and a quick rub with french polish will bring back the warm glow. The new french polishes (e.g., *Lacover* by Mohawk Products, Amsterdam, NY) are not as difficult to use as some would have you believe.

Of course, strippers, stains, wire wheels, etc., in the wrong hands, can result in a nightmare. But that is the fault of the user. Handled properly, wood can be made to light up from within, and iron to reflect the ageless luster of the more noble metals. This can be done without the homogenous horror of heavily polyurethaned wood or the "chromed" look of iron. So the next time someone abhors our techniques, ask him if it is merely because he can't make them work!

We have no desire to convince the purists to change their ways. We recognize their right to collect as they please. But we will never surrender our right to restore an unworkable, lifeless tool into a functionally beautiful and vibrant part of our heritage.

# 8

## CHANCERY SALES
## (1984)

Several years ago I had some fairly active tool sales in a little shop in Chatham, New Jersey. They were always on a Saturday, opened promptly at 9:00 a.m., and had a strict no early-bird rule. But there were complaints that the first half-hour was wild, with frenzied grabbing and in some cases hoarding. It was hard to correct this. I tried to pattern it after Win Carter's sales, as I thought Win was one of the finest gentlemen in the business. But even Win had trouble in this area. So for a number of reasons, including the one above, I stopped my sales and went to auctioning.

This article is not meant to evaluate the difference. Its purpose is to describe an alternative method for a tag sale that provides less need for aggressiveness. It is called a chancery sale (derived from the Court of Equity). It works well and is a great social day to boot. You must, however, set your thinking to accept another culture, almost in another time. The events of this story are basically true; only the names and places have been changed to protect the unbelievable source of supply, which I have dubbed the "Mother Lode."

In an obscure part of England there is a small area of approximately 100 square miles that is poor in soil, poor in industry, and just plain poor. The people, rather than accept the meager welfare available, have taken up crafts (very similar to our Appalachia area). Everyone makes something — some do it well, some not so well. Many have branched out to scavenging antiques from neighboring areas because they have developed a great marketing technique!

Once a month or so, everyone brings their stuff to a huge barn, and they tag everything. About 25 enterprising, but discreet, dealers are invited. Secrecy is everything, as these dealers do not want other people finding out where the Mother Lode is located. And the sellers do not want people from neighboring towns to find their market, or they might start their own sales.

Sale day started with a couple dozen dealers sitting around outside the barn, waiting for opening time. Everyone was socializing, with little regard for jockeying to be the first through the barn doors. Ale and sandwiches were being shared by everyone. Then a hat was passed — not for money, but to pick each dealer's position number. The explanation went like this: In order of pick each man goes in and buys one major and two minor items (predetermined by dollar limit). When everybody has had a turn, they go around again.

Each round was punctuated with hearty gulps of ale. There was absolutely no bargaining inside. Outside, the dealers fiercely traded all their early picks. Sometimes an item changed hands three times.

After about two hours of this, everyone was seemingly "bought out," and turns were being "passed." The barn doors were then closed, and a group of townspeople made their way into the barn via the back door. They were the owners, and their job was to lower prices on things that did not sell. In a few minutes the excitement of purchasing started all over again with the ritual of the sequence-pick being strictly adhered to.

In an hour or so, the doors were closed again and the prices marked down once more (now I know where the Sims' commercial got the idea of price cutting). The basic game plan was that no one — buyer or seller — was to leave before every stick of everything was out of the barn. If you left early, you would not be invited back. Improperly high prices were pressured downward by the seller's peers in an effort to go home. And many magnanimous buyers bought the low-end merchandise just to help out (and also to get home).

But when the day was over, buyers were happy, sellers were happy, and everyone was tipsy. I'm not sure about the tipsy part, but there is an awful lot to be said for the rest.

**"I told you not to hang your stupid plumb bobs on the Christmas Tree!"**

# 9

## A TAKE-APART TREASURE
## (1994)

On occasion, some of my stories about finding tool treasures have been greeted with doubtful looks. I suppose someone who writes tongue-in-cheek articles has to be prepared for this treatment. However, just recently I ran into a typical storytelling piece — but this time it was in the presence of an impeccable witness. I can let it all out on this one, without fear of being accused of coloring-up.

It was the day of the fall Waterloo Show, and it looked like rain. This meant to me that fast walking was required before the downpour. I hadn't been inside the show gate more than a few minutes when I met Steve Orbine (a fellow CRAFTSman). It was a slightly tentative moment for me because Steve is not the hyper "run-through-quick-at-first" type that I am, and I didn't want to be impolite and just buzz off. So I decided to hack along with him for a bit and play it by ear.

The pickings were bad, and I preferred to socialize with Steve rather than rush through. So we just bumped along, complaining about the lack of buyable tools. In desperation, Steve mentioned that he did see a plow plane at a reasonable price, but it was in terrible shape. Any port in a storm was my philosophy at that point, and off we went to see the plow plane.

Terrible shape was a fair appraisal: one main nut split in two, the other cracked wide open; both flat nuts frozen; half the dirt and grime taken off (worse looking than if none of it was removed); rust on all the iron; oxidation on all the brass; and to rub salt in the wound, the entire plane was coated with polyurethane without disassembly. As cheap as it was, and as bad as I wanted to buy something, I passed.

After an hour or so, it started to rain and Steve and I took refuge in one of the tents near where the plow plane was. I just had to take another look, for so far I had bought zilch. The rain and the lack of success in selling anything panicked the dealer into giving me a price that I couldn't refuse. I rationalized that I could make restoration wages on it, so it wouldn't be a loser.

The restoration proceeded better than planned. The poly came right off with steelwool. The nuts glued back together with almost no visible seams. The rust and oxidation polished out without pitting, and the frozen flat nuts popped loose easily. The round brass plugs on the left side of the body fell out when I removed the skate screws. I originally thought they were decoration inserts; and would clean up to give the plane that *special look*. But why would anyone go to the trouble of insetting five round nuts with two anti-rotational wings on each? (See photo.) Wood screws hold just as well or better. (In many restorations the wood screws are so locked in place that they have to be flamed out!) No, it couldn't be for better holding power, nor for decoration. I gave up trying to solve it, but decided not to sell it until I learned more.

A day or two later, in a random conversation with Chuck Granick (another CRAFTSman), I mentioned the plane. It struck a chord with Chuck and he searched through piles of catalogs trying to find it. And find it he did! In Catalog #12 of *The Mechanick's Workbench* (1981), there is an English plane with the same configuration. It was believed that the nuts were to allow the skate to be replaced with a compassed one so as to do coach work. It was handsomely priced because of this rare feature.

**Left side, showing rearmost skate screw and nut removed.**

We also found confirming information of the above, in addition to a full page of another English plane of this type, in Ken Roberts' book *Some 19th Century English Woodworking Tools* (1980). The plane was listed as a "Combination Plough for Straight and Circular Work by Joseph Marples, York Works, Sheffield." In both the Roberts' book and the catalog, the illustrated planes were without the circular or compassed skates, probably lost through lack of use.

The aficionados that I have talked to can't remember seeing many planes like this, and any that they remember were English. Here now is an American convertible-skate plane by *A & E Baldwin / Warranted* (in itself a mark not yet in Pollak's book). Not a bad find on a rainy day with almost nothing to pick from.

Sure, go ahead, call it dumb luck.

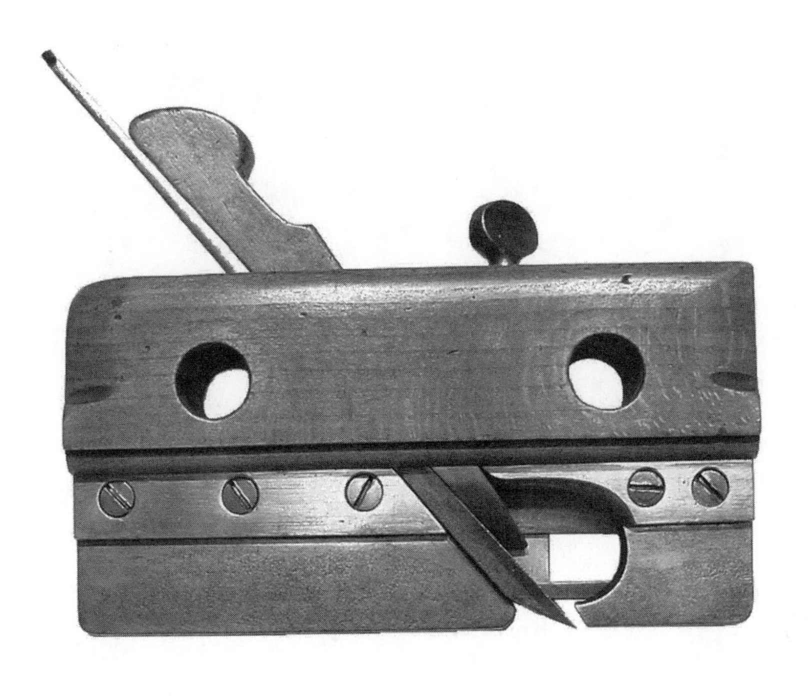

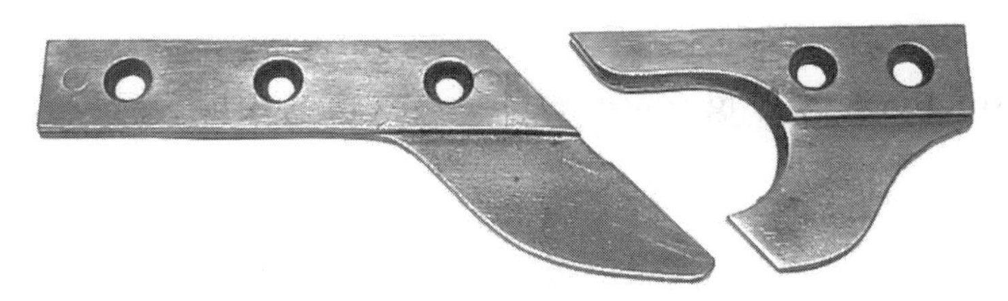

**Right side (fence removed), showing straight and compassed skates. (Compassed skate not original to this plane.)**

# 10

## THE HISTORY OF TOOLS
## (1996)

*Excerpts from the 9 pages written by the author for the encyclopedia,* The New Book Of Knowledge.

The ability to use tools is one of the significant differences between man and the animals. Although some animals use sticks and stones to aid in simple tasks, they have not progressed beyond that. Man, however, developed axes, hammers, knives and drills *over 10,000 years ago*! Tools also played an important part in the making of fire — a turning point in man's development. The improvement of our "creature comforts" is directly related to the tools available to produce these things. Unfortunately, tools have also provided the weapons of war, from the wooden club to the atomic bomb. We are what we are today because of the discoveries that have been put into effect by tools.

There are several periods of our civilization where tools underwent important changes. These "Tool Periods" are described below in a *general* sense, recognizing that there were overlaps in time between some of these periods, and that they did not occur at exactly the same time throughout the world. At best, they are approximations.

## Stone-Age Tool Period
## (10,000 B.C. to 4,000 B.C.)

Although man has been said to have used simple sticks and stones to help him get food since 1,000,000 B.C., it wasn't until around 10,000 B.C. that there is any evidence of simple tools as we know them.

The first **hammers** were probably no more than stones that fit easily into the hand. They were used mostly to break up firewood and shape other tools. The likelihood is that hammers, as with other tools, did not have handles until later in the period. **Scrapers** were small stones chipped sharp on one side, that were used to remove the bits of flesh from the hides that were used for clothing. To put the holes in these hides so as to lace them up with rawhide, **awls** were used. They were needlelike pieces of bone or antler. **Drills** that made holes in wood, and sometimes even in stone, were shaped from long stones that were chipped to a sharp point. Later in their development, these drill points were lashed to a slender shaft and spun between the driller's palms.

To cut and shape wood, stones were chipped into **chisels** — thin flat stones sharpened on the front edge, **gouges** — similar looking but semi-circular and hollow, **knives** — made from a sharply fractured rock or one that was chipped sharp on one side, and **axes** — similar to hammers but sharpened on the striking edge. At a later point these axe heads were lashed to handles, giving the user much more force in the blow. **Adzes** had their chisel-like cutting stones lashed to handles also.

The **saw** was an ingenious tool of the period. It was a long flat stone with teeth chipped into it. In some rare cases the blades were made from volcanic glass. See Fig. 1.

## Copper and Bronze-Age Tool Period
## (4000 B.C. to 1000 B.C.)

There was a great change in tools when man first discovered how to smelt copper (by melting the raw metal from the rock that contained it). Now he could cast the shape of the tool by pouring the molten copper into a clay mold. This yielded a stronger and more precise tool.

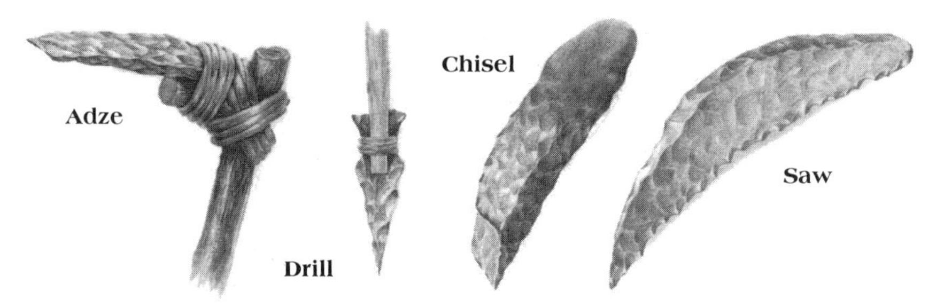


**Fig. 1. Stone Age Tool Period**

Around 3000 B.C. a refinement to copper was discovered. When tin was added to the molten copper, the new material, bronze, was harder than either the tin or the copper! In addition to changing his stone tools to copper or bronze, the toolmaker could now make flat sawblades for **hand saws**. Some of these saws had jewels for teeth, and could cut the hardest of the stone blocks. He could also make **files** to shape and smooth the wood for more precision fits. The **bowdrill** was introduced during this period. It used a more refined drill shaft. The added bow had its rawhide thong wrapped around the drill shaft so as to turn the shaft clockwise and counterclockwise, alternately, with each forward and back stroke.

As many of the works of art and structures of the Egyptians required measurements, the **rule** was developed. The standard unit of Egyptian measurement was the cubit (approximately 27 inches long). The biblical cubit was designated as the distance from the fingertip to the elbow. It was divided into seven palms, with each palm further divided into four digits. All of these markings were scribed onto a wooden or bronze ruler.

Considering the secret passageways that were in the pyramids, and the fact that some of the stones opened these passages by means of a gravity balance, it was necessary for these stones to be perfectly level. This was accomplished by use of a **plumb bob**. A plumb bob was nothing more than a weight on a string that hung straight down due to gravity. When the surface being leveled was exactly perpendicular to the string, that surface was considered level. Although the

Romans are credited with perfecting the **square** to determine a right angle, the Egyptians were the first to use this tool. The Egyptians also used a level in the form of a wooden letter "A". A plumb bob hung from the center point of the "A". When the string crossed the center piece of the "A" exactly at the middle mark, the surface was perfectly level. See Fig. 2.

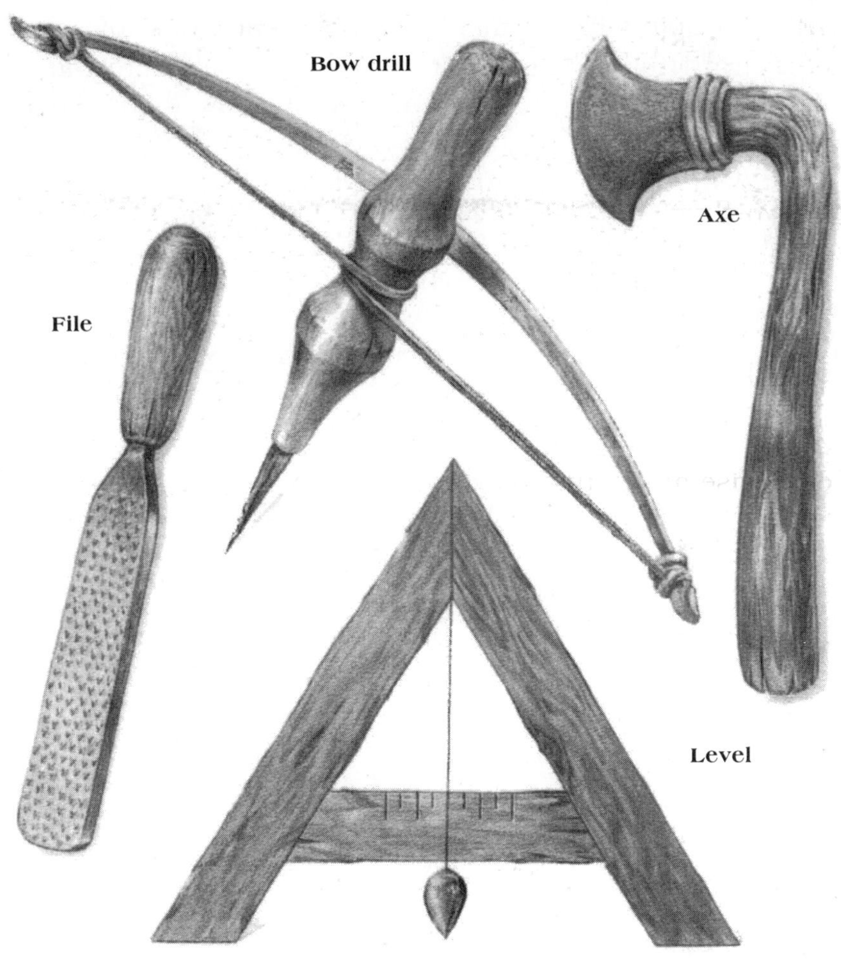


**Fig. 2. Copper and Bronze Age Tool Period**

## Iron-Age Tool Period
## (1000 B.C. to 5th Century A.D.)

Iron tools of this period are primarily of Roman origin. The iron gave greater life to the blades of the tools, and made it easier to do precision work.

Another achievement of this period was the **plane**. It was a vast improvement over the chisel. Its blade was wedged into a wooden block that controlled the depth of the cut. Tight joints for cabinetry work were now possible.

During this period a few new specialty tools were added. Most notable was the **drawknife**, that allowed the woodworker to cut away large quantities of wood with just a few controlled strokes. (Drawknives traced to this period show their handles at 90 degrees to the flat of the blade, an awkward positioning that was changed later.) Another innovation was the **framed saw**, which gave better control to the long "whippy" blades of iron. A third was the **claw hammer** that could extract nails. (Iron nails were first used by the Romans.) Many of these ancient tools are not very different from the ones that we use today. See Fig. 3.

**Fig. 3. Iron Age Tool Period**

## Medieval Tool Period
## (5th Century A.D. to 16th Century A.D.)

This period covered the Dark Ages, Middle Ages, and Renaissance. There were very few changes in what the Romans had set up in the way of tools, until the 15th and 16th century Renaissance. At that time **planes** took over as the preferred tool, and many modifications to them were made. Also **boring tools** were developed. **Augers**, **reamers**, and **bit braces** became the prime tools for boring, even though bowdrills were used well into the 19th century. Axe heads changed their style during this period; they became more flared. See Fig. 4.

Barrelmaking, called coopering, depended upon craftsmen that had both strength and skill. Although barrels were made by the Romans, production techniques didn't improve very much until this period. One of the largest woodworking tools was the Cooper's Long Jointer Plane for shaping staves. It reached 6 to 8 feet in length and about 5" by 5" in

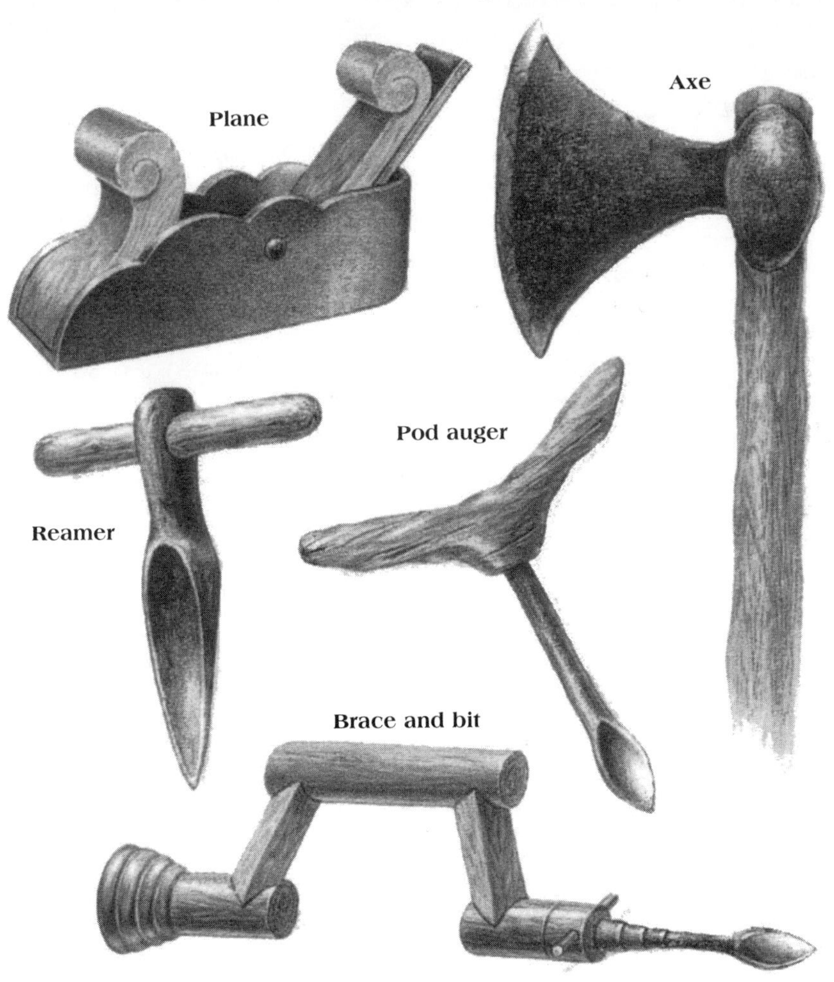


**Fig. 4. Medieval Tool Period**

cross-section — too heavy for a man to push. So, the plane was turned upside down (blade up), and the cooper pushed the barrelstave over the blade of the plane, instead of the usual technique of running the plane over the work.

### Transitional Tool Period (17th and 18th Century A.D.)

This was the time that toolmaking became a separate trade, and masters trained apprentices in shops mostly centered in the industrial area of England, and to some extent the northeastern United States. It wasn't until the late 1600's that English planemakers started to sign their tools. The first recorded American planemaker was Francis Nicholson of Wrentham, Massachusetts. His working years are estimated between 1716 and 1753.

As fancy architecture and ornate furniture became more and more desirable, artisan's skills and their tools improved. **Molding planes** were developed to cut the profiles of the trim pieces that were used in the homes and on the furniture of the period. Planes were made that could cut grooves and joints for better fits; one such example was the **plow plane**. The saw blades were made thinner so that veneer could be used on furniture.

Steel was now being made in England and because it was still very scarce, only small pieces were forged onto the edge of iron cutting blades, which greatly improved the sharpness and life of the blade.

**Broad axes**, which were used to hew the beams for the great houses and barns, became a common tool of the 18th century. **Braces** in this period were made larger and stronger and along with **augers** and **reamers** were used in construction of ships, bridges and buildings. Blacksmiths were improving their skills also, and during the 18th century they were able to make a **brace** completely of iron. Tools and the men who used them, came into their own during this period. Although these tools were still crude in comparison to those to come in the 19th century, they were sufficient to produce some magnificent pieces of furniture. See Fig. 5.

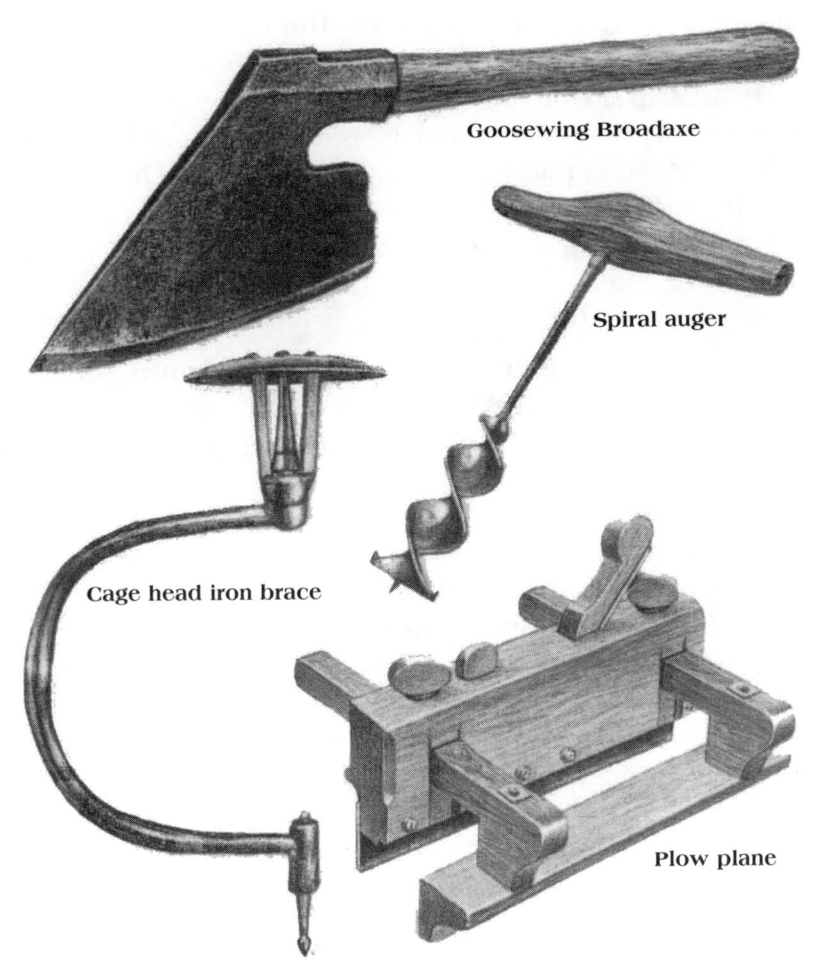


Fig. 5. Transitional Tool Period

## Industrial Tool Period (19th Century A.D.)

The 1800s were the years when hand-made tools produced by a single craftsman gave way to tools made in large shops and factories by many varied craftsmen. The Industrial Age provided an explosion of tools, without which many new products would not have been available.

Foundries were now able to **cast** iron, instead of the laborious task of hand forging it with hammers. This ability provided planemakers with the opportunity to make their planes completely out of iron. By the end of the century, iron planes had just about made the wooden ones obsolete.

**Standardization** was another concept that started in the 19th century. It resulted in parts that could be interchanged between manufacturers, and reduced the need for so many different sizes of the same tool.

**Specialization** and **assembly-line techniques** did not occur until late in the 19th century, but once they did, America became the foremost tool producer in the world.

### Modern Tool Period
### ( 20th Century AD)

Many of the tools used today are not that different from those produced in the 1800's. The most significant difference has been in the development of electric power tools. However, the modern period has also seen the development of automated machines and robots, some operated by computers. In many factories, the entire production process is automated, and computer programs tell the machines exactly what to do.

Tools continue to play an important role in our lives because we depend on them to help us accomplish many important tasks. The versatility of today's tools has also enabled millions of people to do work that only skilled craftspeople could do in the past.

# 11

## THE FLORIDA CAPER (1995)

Last February I went to Florida to see a lifelong friend who was quite ill. I realized that I had to do something to keep my mind off a rather sorrowful situation. So I decided to walk the beaches at night and hit the flea markets and antique shops in the morning, both times when my friend would be asleep. I didn't expect much in the way of tools from the area, but it was the "hunt" that would help distract me from the problem.

It was 40 miles from the Florida airport to where I was going and I decided to take Route 1 rather than the Interstate. I have nostalgic memories of Route 1. As a boy I hitchhiked from my home in New Jersey to Canada, and at a later time to Key West. Both times I used Route 1. They were great adventures, and I have always felt a kinship with this road. Besides, it holds more antique shops and flea markets per mile than most other roads.

Arriving in Florida directly from a New Jersey snowstorm tends to brighten one's spirits. It was the equivalent of a gorgeous spring day back home, and I started to shake off the gloom associated with the trip. I was only a few miles from the airport when I hit my first "junk shop." It was deliciously awful, like the places I used to go to before Doris convinced me that better tools were usually in better shops.

However, I couldn't resist going in. What the heck, Doris was over a thousand miles away.

I was surprised at what I found. There actually were tools there, and some of them were useable. Only one was collectible, but the price reflected that fact. I picked up the lone goody and mused over it a while. With my Jersey accent, rental-car plates, and expensive shoes, I wasn't in a good negotiating position, but the proprietor made me an offer I couldn't refuse. He also gave me a good lay-of-the-land for shops that might yield tools.

I followed his instructions to the next shop. Although it was much farther than, "jist down the road a bit," I found it. Not much was there, but I didn't despair. Two shops later, my trip to Florida was almost paid for! I couldn't believe it. I didn't stop to analyze the situation; I just grabbed and ran. Some things were priced so high that they took my breath away. Others were dirt cheap. Because my plan was to take only things that would fit easily into my suitcase, I left a few good bargains. Even so, the suitcase was getting filled to the brim, and I knew I would have to borrow another.

After arriving at my friend's house, I needed to find something for us to do that didn't take much effort. Because of his previous activity in the flea markets in the area, he became interested in my tool buys. He asked me to lay the stuff on the floor so he could vicariously participate in the purchases. I detected a sadness in his voice when he told me about the early morning flea markets, as he knew he couldn't go. He hadn't been out of the house in over a month, and his wife told me that he could never make it down the front steps.

I went alone to the markets the next morning. They proved similar to the shops, mostly tourist prices, but many mistakes. I could understand the mistakes as “a little knowledge is a dangerous thing,” but I couldn't figure out where all these tools were coming from. Finally I asked. This was the answer: It was a retirement area and the recession had seriously hurt the retirees. So, many collections from the “old days” were sold to help bridge the problem.

Both the dealers and the retired "closet" collectors were aware of the increase in tool prices since the old days, but they did not have enough current experience to price properly. I envied the knowledgeable collectors in the area as I knew they must have gotten some pretty good bargains.

However, guilt started to swell up in my psyche. I felt that some of these guys needed the money. But I knew someone who needed it more, so I decided to use the profits to help my friend. A new vibrancy took over, and I now pursued the hunt with a vengeance. I returned home for breakfast each morning with boxes of stuff. The excitement that my friend displayed over my finds was more therapeutic than the myriad of drugs that he had to take every few hours. He decided that he was going to try the stairs, and with our help he might make it to the car. HE DID! We rode around the shoreline for awhile and returned home. A fatigued but rejuvenated person flopped into his bed that night. He had more hope than he had for the past months. In the next few days he was up and around good enough to go to a restaurant!

The story should end here, but I have to relate an incident at the airport. I decided to take one of the more valuable tool suitcases as a carry-on. I knew it might cause some trouble through the "X-ray" machine, but I wanted to see how effective that operation was. They picked it up all right, and with a gasp the operator called her supervisor. He tried to keep from frightening everyone, but he must have been new and was unable to hide his concern. I tried to explain what those ominous-looking things on the screen were, but to no avail.

Another security guard (this one with sidearm) was quickly called, and he directed me to, "Open up." I noticed everyone slowly moving away as I opened the case to remove the tools. The first piece I grabbed was a Bedrock 603. The guard knew it was a plane and relaxed, but every single piece still had to be laid out on a table in plain view. People in a hurry flew by, but those who had time gathered around to browse. The guard started to ask questions, not concerning security, but to satisfy his curiosity about the tools.

Never let it be said that I would fail to put on a tool demonstration, no matter where! There was quite a crowd, maybe only a minute or two for each, but there was still a lot of interest.

All-in-all the Florida trip was highly successful. I like to think that most of the success was due to antique tools.

**"When the doctor told Marvin to exercise more, he took up tool collecting."**

# 12

## SOMETIMES IT PAYS TO BE A PACKRAT (1995)

My wife (and many others) asks the same question year in and year out about my boxes of "spare parts" and miscellaneous hardware, "Why are you saving all that junk, you never use it?" The answer is always the same, "I might." And, on semi-rare occasions I do use it. But most of the time it just sits there gathering dust and building up my guilt for using needed space. During a recent holiday, I had a chance to finally demonstrate something positive that came from saving "things." My son Steve had brought home a box of tools that either: 1) he couldn't sell in Maine, 2) needed fixing, or 3) just were getting in his way. My job, "should I accept it," as they used to say on "Mission Impossible," was to turn this box of junk into something of value. My son must have inherited my packrat complex, because before he could take anything to the dump he would bring it home "for Dad." My first reaction to such a box was to complain bitterly, but before long I was rummaging through, picking out this and that, and saving things that I knew I would use — someday.

Once in a while, to make a point, I would make a big scene over a piece that was just completely worthless. It was to keep Steve on his toes, I guess. Such a piece was in the latest box. It was a body of a smoothing plane, just the body

— no wedge or iron. The top of the body was severely burned over an area of two or three square inches. The sole was gouged out here and there, and the inlay to the mouth (to narrow the opening) was gone. On top of all this it was covered with paint speckles and grease. If I were to dream up a worthless tool, I couldn't improve on this one. There was not one saving grace about it, no signature, nothing.

It was a perfect specimen to unleash my tirade about saving junk, even though I was guilty myself. I thought I could make a few points with Doris by expounding on the necessity to scrap things when they are worthless. Steve, who had heard the speech before, just weathered through it with as little shifting of weight as possible. When I was finished, I started to chuck the plane in the trash can when I heard, "I thought you could use the wood for ebony inlays."

"Ebony! Haven't I taught you anything about wood? Look how open the grain is, it's not ebony."

"What is it?"

"Uh, its probably one of those heavy mahoganies, Cuban maybe."

"Isn't that worth saving?"

"If it means that much to you I'll save it," I mumbled. But my mind was already racing ahead to when I could get the piece off to myself and find out what the wood really was.

I knew it wasn't Cuban mahogany; in fact I wasn't sure it was mahogany at all. At my first opportunity I took it over to the band saw to cut a cross section. But I couldn't do it! What if it were a truly exotic wood? Then the plane would certainly be worth restoring. I decided to just cut the burn off the top and the tears off the sole and see what the exposed wood was. Was I ever surprised. It was wenge! (Some pronounce it "whenj," but because the word originally carried an accent over the second e, most call it "when-gay," a cross between the French and the American versions.) Wenge is a very abrasive-resistant wood that works well with tools and remains stable. If I were to make a plane that had to take a lot of abuse, I would make it out of wenge. I know of no factory-made planes using this wood, and know of only a few others that were probably made by ship-builders. We are now talking about a rare tool, at least rare in my definition.

When everyone left after the holiday, I restored it with an ebony inlay at the mouth, and a nicely chamfered ebony wedge. After the crud was taken off, the irregularly swirled shades of brown and black grain, with a hint of reddish brown from the freshly-cut areas, were gorgeous. I was quite proud of myself, but there was one perplexing issue still unresolved: how to explain all this to my son after the speech I gave him.

He is a member of CRAFTS and gets the *Tool Shed.* I'll let this article take care of the explanation. Sorry Steve.

**"Would you like to come up to my place and see my antique tools?"**

# 13

## HOW ARE YOU COVERED?
## (1980)

What is the second most valuable thing you own? You might be surprised to find that it is your tool collection.

Yes, more valuable than your car, or your wife's diamond ring, or even your furniture.

But is the collection properly insured? Most people don't know, and the rest freely admit that some coverage is lacking. Tools will burn as easily as furniture or oil paintings, but they are usually treated as country cousins when it comes to insurance coverage. I think this is because collectors feel the cost and effort would be prohibitive. Not so!

Antique tools are not *specifically* limited under the personal property section of your homeowners policy. Therefore, within the general limits of that section (one-half the value of your house) you are covered. Even if your collection (in total with your other personal property) exceeds the general limit you can increase the limit for about $2 annual premium per thousand dollars of collection. This is paid only against the *excess*.

A more expensive but far better coverage is a separate Fine Arts Floater. Its advantages are:

1. There is no deductible.

2. “All risk” is offered, rather than the specific “named perils” of the usual homeowners policy.

3. Your entire collection, or any part of it, is covered off your premises — at tool meetings, displays, etc.

4. And last but most important, you can have each tool insured for a predetermined “stated amount” rather than the vague “actual cash value” of most homeowners policies.

To have coverage is one thing, to properly collect is another. One simple way that precludes any problem is to prove in advance that you have the tool and that its stated value is correct. This requires an inventory (a few composite photos are a big help). Copies of your inventory sheets are sent to the insurance company and updated whenever you like.

You can have them approved by an appraiser of your choice (any recognized tool dealer will do), or you can offer your collection “open to audit.” I elect the latter and have recent catalogs available to cross-check prices. However, the likelihood is that you will never see an auditor. Many insurance companies consider antique collectors good “moral risks” and will accept their inventories without audit.

So for a day or two of effort, if you don't already have an inventory, you can rest easy about insuring your collection. True, insurance cannot guarantee against the loss of your treasures, but at least it gives you the option of replacing them properly.

# 14

## WHIMSICAL TALE
## (1983)

I recently took a trip to England and came back with a great tool story. It was told to me by a renowned Englishman one sunny afternoon as we sat in his shop sipping tea. For the most part, there was an impish twinkle in his eye, but at times he maintained a serious, prideful bearing. It goes like this:

When Victoria became Queen of England in the mid-1800s, she was young and not completely experienced in matters of domestic policy. She had many advisors and court politicians, but she wanted to do something special for the people, all on her own. It wasn't long before she got her chance.

The Carpenter's Guild sent its Chief Steward to see her about reducing the seventy-hour work week. She was surprised to hear that anyone had to work such long hours. But her advisors convinced her that if she made any changes with the carpenters, then the bakers, silversmiths, etc., would all be camped on her throne-step for similar easements and the entire economy of the kingdom would collapse.

What a dilemma! Here was Victoria, wanting to do something to show her appreciation for her crafts people, but not wishing to anger her lordly advisors. What to do? It all came to her in the proverbial flash. She recalled her favorite fairy tale, about a King who offered his daughter's hand to the craftsman who could mold the most perfect golden frog.

As the tale goes, craftsmen came from far and wide to try their luck at sculpting a golden frog. But to no avail. The King turned them all down as imperfect. Finally a brilliant technician-type figured out that if he used a real frog as an actual model and cast around it, he could make a perfect likeness. And by utilizing what is known today as the lost-wax process, he created a flawless golden frog. The King was delighted and gave the young suitor his daughter's hand in marriage and half his kingdom. Of course, the King kept the thousands of rejected golden frogs and was understandably elated with his new found fortune.

Victoria found the fairy tale a solution to her dilemma. She announced to her kingdom that the craftsman who made the most perfect brass-framed ebony brace would become Master of the Queen's Carpenters and would be granted the prestigious Queen's Letters. She described the brace as the ultimate in tools and called it an "Ultimatum" for short.

There were many applicants, just like in the fairy tale. All submitted their samples — men like Pasley, Howarth, Marsden, Marples, Flather, Sorby, Ridge, Kent, and so on. After much deliberation, she picked the brace made by William Marples, and he became an overnight celebrity. The Queen awarded him a large patent citation with her letters embossed in gold, and he was allowed to advertise this honor on his subsequent braces with the inscription: "By Her Majesty's Royal Letters Patent."

Strange as it may seem, the original complaint by the Carpenter's Guild was quickly resolved. Queen Victoria reached an agreement with the Chief Steward that each of the royal carpenters would receive one of the left-over contest braces in lieu of a reduction of work hours. All was well again in the kingdom and most certainly for William Marples who lived happily ever after, making his "Ultimatums."

And that is why today, of all the brass-framed ebony braces that have made their way to the "colonies," only one type carries the Queen's seal of approval — the Ultimatum by William Marples.

Note: Please, no letters on any anachronisms or literary liberties taken in this story. Just enjoy it for what it is — a tall-tool-tale.

**"Did ya 'ear? The Queen is recalling all the ULTIMATUMS due to a manufacturing defect."**

# 15

## A CRASH COURSE ON HANDLE MAKING (1979)

Although this article is concerned with making handles, I hope it goes beyond that for the non-woodworking reader. The making of handles, wedges and other small wooden parts provides an entry into woodworking that is within the scope of most people's talent and equipment. If you are strictly a tool collector, and never had a passion to try your hand at the skills of the trade, then this article is for you. Almost every collector, at one time or another, reflects upon how well a tool will cut. For some, that is where it ends — as a reflection. But just about anyone can be a handlemaker!

To start with, you don't need much money or experience — just a few tools and some stock. Many primitive handlemakers had no lathes, and we will follow in their footsteps. You will need, however, a few saws, a drawknife, a small chisel, some files, and an all-important vise (smoking or drinking won't do!). A grinding wheel is almost a necessity. You can use a small hand wheel, but it is much better to put a wheel on a salvaged appliance motor.

You will have to sharpen your tools more often than usual, as most handles are made from tough stock (hickory, ash, and rock maple). Sharpening is an art, and is quite satisfying when you get it right. It can be frustrating if you don't give it enough concentration. The trick is to keep from "turning over the edge," i.e., inadvertently twisting the blade from its proper angle so that you cut off the very edge you have worked so hard to get.

The sharpening angle determines the ease of entry into the wood. An acute angle starts the blade better, but will dull or chip quicker. Even so, the more acute angle is best for the beginner, as it affords greater accuracy with the tool. If your sharpening is right, you should *feel* no burr, *see* no edge shine, and be able to *shave* the hair on the back of your wrist (if you're hairless, you will never be a handlemaker).

Your first project should be something easy, like fitting an old handle to that great axe head that has been laying around for years. Old handles can be bought cheaply at flea markets. Start your fitting by marking out any large amounts of wood that have to be removed. This is best done by saw. Now start shaping-in with the drawknife. At this point you will undoubtedly run into the phenomenon of the "run-of-the-grain." When the grain runs out, i.e., is slightly diagonal to the surface you are working, the tool will dig-in in one direction and cut smoothly in the other. See Fig. 1. Sharp tools and fine craftsmen can cut in either direction, but I suggest that the beginner learn early how to turn the tool around to cut "with the run."

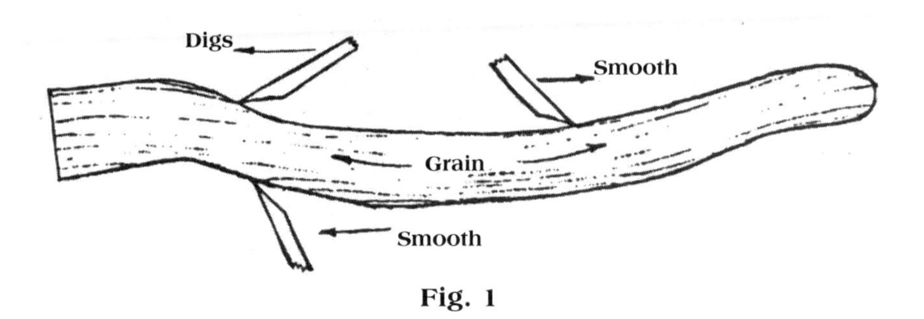


**Fig. 1**

The handle can be smoothed-in or finished with the spoke shave and block plane, melding the new cuts with the old body. It can be filed and scraped to blend in the patina. If a wedge is required, one can be cut with a dovetail saw and flushed off after being driven. If you make a few small mistakes and take too much stock in some areas of the eye, drive some fill wedges in these "holes." If you really louse up, cut off the head and use the remaining handle for a hatchet head.

After you have cut a few axe wedges, try your hand at plane wedges. They are not really hard, and they can put new life into an otherwise functionless tool. The stock is easy to get from old plane bodies that are missing all their parts and are sold as scrap. A few jointers cut up can make a pile of wedges. If you don't care about the age of the wood, you can get all kinds of small pieces at any lumberyard that carries hardwoods.

First, plane the stock to width and thickness. Then make a layout of the angle and cut it out of cardboard. Adjust for fit, then cut your wedge. If you have some wedges in other planes that fit, you can save all the trouble of making a template — just trace the wedge that works. A coping saw and some files will "round-in" the knockout portion of the wedge. Make sure you do the knockout portion last, leaving plenty of extra stock.

Now you are ready for your first creative handle — the broad axe. The proper way is to cut the stock from an already bent piece (which is difficult to get in a seasoned condition) or steam bend it (which is also difficult with meager equipment). So we will cut the bend angle into the stock by starting with a piece thick enough to accommodate this angle. Surprisingly enough, a pick-axe handle is thick enough to give you a couple of inches of "sway." Mark out your cuts and rip saw out the bulk. See Fig. 2. Then fit the head as you did previously with the drawknife and plane. Shave, file smooth and wedge up. Most primitive broad axes were wedged between the eye and the handle, rather than down a slit in the handle as are the modern axes.

If you have done well on the broad axe, keep your eye out for a goosewing without a handle — preferably foreign, as they have larger eyes. For stock, use an old wagon axle or tongue. There is a lot of this stuff around in barn sales and junk shops, once you start looking for it. Remember not

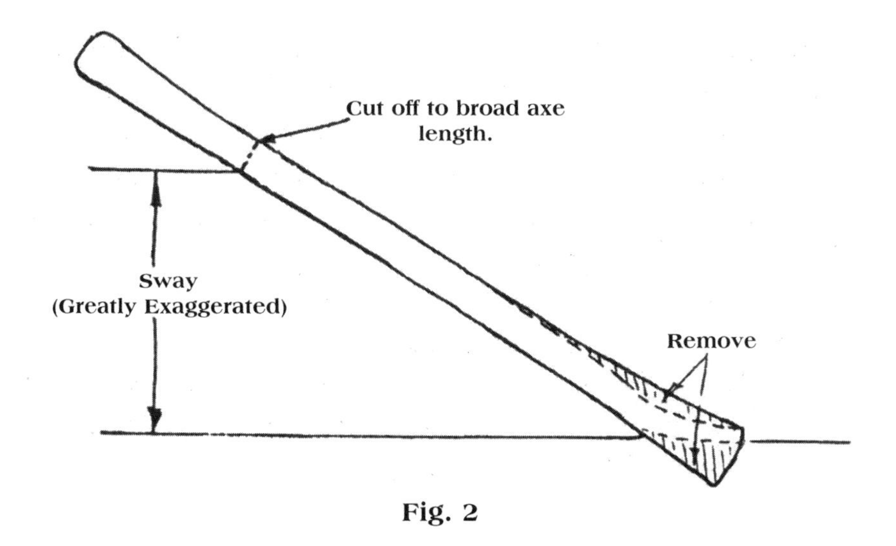


**Fig. 2**

to take the rust off the inside of the eye as you can use it as an indicator of the high spots. There is a lot of trial and error to making this handle, but you'll be proud when it is finished and it looks the part.

The piece-de-resistance of handle making is the American goosewing with its 3/16 inch eye. But how many of us are fortunate enough to get a good American goosewing, even without a handle? If you do, remember to make a couple of cardboard inside templates before you start. It will cut down the trial-and-error tremendously.

Chisels and draw knives can be rehandled with round stock, shaped with a drawknife and drilled in steps to achieve a tapered hole for the tang of the chisel. Slicks or socket chisels can be handled from old table legs, baseball bats or large implement handles. The difference between a workman-like job and a "botch" is the taper of the socket portion. This should be measured with a pair of calipers, and the diameters transferred to the handle stock. Don't jam in a tapered handle without shouldering it first. This can be done with a dove-tail saw and a chisel (see Figure 3). Make the "L" length slightly shorter on the handle, so it doesn't "bottom." Be sure that the overall diameter "D" of the end of the socket is the same on the handle where you start your shoulder cut. Cut down no deeper than the

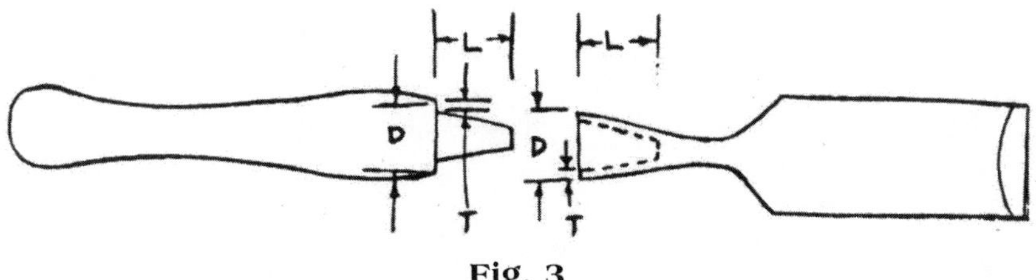


**Fig. 3**

thickness of the socket "T." Chisel out the taper and smooth with a drawknife. File down so that when lightly pushing the handle into the socket there is about 1/8 inch between the socket and the shoulder of the handle. Then ram the handle home. If it is too loose, put thin wood shavings in the socket and ram it home again. Wrap tape around the socket to keep from breaking the patina of the iron if you miss with the file, and file the handle so that it becomes an exact extension of the socket. Then stand back and admire your work!

Handle and wedge making can do wonders for your collection, and you might get to really enjoy it. It is no disgrace to refit a head or an iron. This is exactly what the craftsmen of yesterday would have done — and in many cases actually did. The satisfaction of putting a fine tool in working condition is on a par with owning the tool itself.

# 16

## PRIORITIES
## (1987)

The other day I was rummaging around in the attic, and I came upon an old window fan that brought back memories.

It was the summer of '78 and it was a hot one. Doris had rented a small cottage on Lake St. Catherine in western Vermont, and we were packing for our one week stay. I had trouble staying more than one week at any one place, as I was more interested in tool-hunting than fishing or boating. As we were going on-the-road for an additional week after St. Catherine, Doris had to fill the wagon with clothes for "possible" places. I was at the height of my Saturday Sales and wanted to come back with enough stuff for a great sale in September.

So, the argument started. Why is this needed, and can't you leave those shoes home? I didn't win any part of the argument (even though my logic was overwhelmingly superior). At one point I suggested that as the lake was a cool spot, we ought to leave the large bulky window fan at home. The only thing cool at that point was her look. The fan remained in the station wagon.

Our stay at the lake was not one of our better ones, but that is another story. What helped for me was a run up to Vern Ward's old place near Lake Bomoseen. Vern was cleaning up his back room; and we struck a deal for the stuff that was "in the way." However, there was one major problem. There were so many more tools than I had expected, I could not fit them all in and still have room for the suitcases and clothes back at the cottage. Vern wondered what the fan was doing in the wagon. It certainly was cool enough the past few weeks. He agreed to hold it for me until the next trip up, and that settled the problem. (We both forgot about it, and I didn't take it back until years later.)

We left the cottage a few days earlier than planned and decided to use the time to go all the way up to Jonesport, Maine, and visit the Jonesport Tool Co. I had heard that they had all kinds of tools, new and old. Doris hadn't noticed the missing fan, and I was sure that Maine would be cool near the water.

Traveling on US 1 in Maine was terrific in those days (as long as you didn't go too far beyond Bar Harbor). Route 1 was both a tourist road and a mecca for tool dealers. Even today, towns like Ogunquit, Wells, Kennebunk, Arundel, Freeport, Wiscasset, Damariscotta, Camden, Lincolnville, and Searsport have shops and fleas that are loaded with tools. Not top-notch tools, but at least something to pick over.

The Jonesport Tool Co. was somewhat disappointing — probably because I over-anticipated. So, rather than stay in Jonesport (which I don't think has a motel anyway), we started back and stopped at Cherryfield around suppertime. Cherryfield is in the cranberry country and generally humid. It is also 40 miles from anywhere.

That day the temperature reached way beyond the norm and the humidity was one point from a downpour. I don't think I have to tell you that the motel had no air conditioning or even a fan. And of course, Doris wanted to know what happened to our fan. It looked bleak for me at that point. I had nothing left to do but fess-up. As I explained it, the fan was merely a question of *priorities*. Something had to go, back there at Vern's — the fan or the shoes or some tools. It really wasn't a hard choice for me. How about you?

# 17

## THE STANLEY NO. 39$^{13}/_{16}$"
## (1994)

Back in 1985 when John Walter published his little pocket price guide for Stanley planes, he listed the No.39$^{13}/_{16}$" as $2500-5000. It was the most expensive model in his book. I think this was because up to that point very few people had ever seen a $^{13}/_{16}$, and most weren't even sure that Stanley produced such a model. Those who believed that it existed said that there was no identification on the piece.

It was right after the publication of that guide that I heard that one was found. It was in the box, and the box had the identification marks of $^{13}/_{16}$". I'm not sure what it sold for, but in John Walter's next book (1986) he changed the price to $1000-2500, but this included the box. It was not until the fall of 1988 that the $^{13}/_{16}$" rarity was heard from again (at least in a public sale). It sold without the box for $1000 at Bud Brown's auction.

The No.39 dado series was introduced by Stanley around 1900. John Walter puts the $^{13}/_{16}$" model as first coming out in 1921. Stanley probably wanted to give the woodworker a dado that would cut a groove that could exactly accommodate a 1" dressed board, which at that time was planed to $^{13}/_{16}$". It didn't sell. Perhaps because it was necessary to dress the side of the dado groove slightly, and as such the 3/4" was much better suited for the job.

In any case, it was obvious that Stanley was not sure they had a winner, and they coppered their bets by not making a permanent casting. What they probably did was treat the No. 39 13/16" as an experimental model and sent it to their machine shop to have it milled down to size from the 7/8" casting.

Having worked in factories a good part of my life, I can picture what happened next. The machinist proudly showed the finished piece to the sales engineer, who complained about the 7/8" still being on the body. "You told me to make it 13/16", you didn't say anything about milling off any identification," was a likely response from the machinist. He then milled off *No.39.7/8 In* (and not very workmanlike I might add). Now the new product was put on the conference table with all the applicable department heads etc., hovering over it making all kinds of glowing predictions. Finally someone said, "Why did they mill off the No. 39, why not leave that on and just take off the 7/8 In?" "Brilliant," everyone agreed (except the fellow who was competing for the suggestor's job). So another sample went back to the machine shop with plenty of remarks about "those guys in the front office never being able to make up their minds." Finally the altered 13/16" was born and made its way into the marketplace — where it promptly flopped amidst a chorus of "I told you so" from everyone except the poor schnook who thought it up.

Before you give this speculative part of the story a frown, let me tell you that until recently the two pieces that I mentioned, and a few others that showed up, all had the *7/8 In* milled off but not the *No.39*. HOWEVER — I just got a piece that has both the *No.39* and the *7/8 In* milled off. My first reaction was that it was not genuine, but then I wondered why anyone would go to such extremes (there is a lot of precision milling involved) and not follow the look of what existed in the literature, namely that the No.39 is not removed. Then I thought perhaps a woodworker of many years ago wanted a 13/16" and had his machinist friend make it for him. Why then mill off all the identification, and then painstakingly rejapan it perfectly, if its only going into your toolbox?

Without using any of the above arguments as positive, I preceded to investigate further. I felt there had to be stronger evidence than just whether the japanning over the milled spot was original. Remember the entire left side of the piece and all of the grooves on that side had to be remilled also. Before giving you my results, I should offer one piece of information: when metal is milled it leaves telltale minute marks that are as good as fingerprints. Under 5X magnification you can tell the size and feed of the cutter, and even its orientation. You can also detect the tiny tear marks and running lines produced by the cutter. I won't say it's impossible to reproduce these marks and their attendant patina, but I doubt that anybody sloppy enough not to follow the known example would care (or even know) about such facts. And if it was just someone making one for a friend some time back, in no way would the"fingerprints" exactly duplicate the factory-made pieces.

The milling marks on my No.39 13/16" are absolutely identical on both sides. In fact, they even match the lines of the 3/4" and 7/8" pieces. This tends to prove that the entire piece was done in the same set-up with the same cutter etc., and therefore is a factory alteration.

I would like to think that not only do I own a rare plane but I may have the prototype!

# 18

## A WISH COME TRUE
## (1988)

Since retiring, I've had so many different tries at "semi-retirement" that I'm embarrassed to mention them all. About the only thing that could be considered successful is the amassing of knowledge relative to the trials and tribulations of retirement. However, this is not the place for a general article on retirement, so I will restrict this column to my venture that pertains to CRAFT members, namely, the buying and selling of antiques.

Oh yes, I have bought and sold tools for many years, but always for "one day stands," e.g., my old Saturday Sales, an occasional day at Lambertsville, or an auction. I have never had a regular open shop, and I always felt I was missing the best part of the business. I envied the "real" dealers. So, when opportunity presented itself to realize my wish, I jumped at it. I now share expenses with a few other dealers in a co-op antique shop. Each dealer has a specialty, and there is a great spirit of cooperation. That's perfect for me, as I know very little about glass, bric-a-brac, art or the staple of the antique business — furniture. I contribute by helping the other dealers with tools and primitives.

After being exposed to the other facets of antiques, I still maintain that tools are the most fascinating of all collectibles. Almost at the drop of a hat, you can gather a crowd to listen to an explanation of the usage of some old tool or implement. (Getting them to buy is another subject.)

Doris and I fixed up our space, and we felt kinda proud. Harry O'Neill helped me with some of his pieces to fill out the area (450 square feet takes a lot of stuff). My son, Steve, sent me two crates of decoys. We were "real" dealers at last!

The story goes a little downhill from here. The first thing that was driven home to me was an answer to a peculiarity that had bothered me for years. On my old buying trips, I would sometimes try to buy in bulk lots from a dealer, only to be told he was not interested. He explained that he would do better selling piece-by-piece. It's true, the individual pieces might be better, but the end of the year yield (after turning his inventory quicker) would be higher if he bulked it out. I never got very far with this "brilliant" business theory, and it irked me. But it's clear now — if you sell off things, *they have to be replaced.* You just don't pick up the phone and order a few extra widgets for the coming month.

Tools were always easy for me to come by, mostly because of my New England contacts, so I just assumed that all categories of antiques must be somewhat the same. If they are, I've sure been left off on the wrong street corner. Getting stock takes *work*! I see my dealer buddies sleeping in their cars to be early in line for a house sale, sitting through hour after hour of a junk auction to get one or two pieces, and going after wild-goose-chase phone calls time after time.

I also never really gave a lot of thought to the hidden expenses attached to a shop. With an open shop you are nailed to the wall, unless you have help that allows you to get away. If your help is your wife and you don't want to "count" her time, that's one thing; but if you have to hire, that's another. Insurance and taxes take on a different complexion in an open shop. And an ugly monster appears — one that I never saw much of in my previous selling ventures — *theft*, from both pros and kleptos.

Sure there is a good side. That's why I'm still in the shop. Aside from the financial gain, the comraderie of the business is great. It's like sitting around the cracker barrel telling stories, except you make some money at it. At my old Saturday Sales, or at an auction, there never was any time for socializing. I admit there was substantially better income at these functions, but there was very little fun. I now have more time on my hands and so do the customers. I'm sure that I'll reach the point that most dealers reach — where the public is frustrating or painful on occasion; but it goes away and you're all set for another weekend.

It's been written that the easiest way to appreciate someone else's problem is to "walk a mile in their shoes." I've now done that, and my tolerance has greatly increased. With that in mind, I'd like to leave you with a couple of thoughts:

Next time you hear a tale of woe from a knowledgeable dealer, give him the benefit of the doubt.

If you want the luxury of a place to go whenever you take the notion, be prepared to pay slightly higher prices (except, of course, in my shop — what do I care if I lose money?)

# 19

## BRIMFIELD
## (1986)

I'm not sure I have the right title to this story. It's about Brimfield all right, but that's not the real issue. The different styles of antique hunting are probably closer to the core of the matter.

I've been to Brimfield before, and it has always been a first-class happening in my life. The preparation, the reservations, the excitement, the awakening at 4:00 a.m., the scramble, the first load back to the car, the tired feet, and finally the utter exhaustion are all integral parts of Brimfield. I can tell you there have been disappointments (more times than not), rain, hurried mistakes, and some hard feelings generated by the competitiveness. But it never seemed to me that any of these problems could be avoided if one was to really "do Brimfield." Not completely so, as I accidentally found out.

Brimfield is probably the largest gathering of antique dealers anywhere. It stretches from the eastern end of the town, across lawns, in groves, in fields — on both sides of the road — all the way to the far western meadows. There must be over 3,000 dealers at its peak. It also has the unique characteristic of having sections (or markets as they are called) open at different times. Starting Monday morning (three times a year) there is a market-opening every day (except Friday) until Saturday. It gives you the feeling of fresh merchandise no matter when you come, and if you want to stay for a few days, you can have the excitement of a new opening each morning.

The worst possible day would be Friday, as there is no opening that day, and the worst time would be just after lunch — too late for leftovers and too early for the late day "give-aways" before packing up. Yes, you guessed it — that's when we arrived! I won't bore you with the reasons for this untimely arrival, but I was fully aware of the hopelessness of the situation and accepted my fate with no misgivings. Therefore, I decided just to stroll around for an hour or so, see some old friends, and shove off.

The whole idea of "strolling around" was repulsive at first, but it started to grow on me. I actually had time to talk to people and find out information in areas of interest. My eye started to pick up objects besides tools, and I found some excellent buys even at that off-hour. An early Dunhill pirate pistol cigarette lighter really struck my fancy, and we had fun bargaining over whether the front legs could be re-bent back without breaking them. A goat's head bronze hammer was stuck in a box of junk and made a great buy. I bought a few unusual wrenches for Frank Kingsbury because I had time to study their mechanisms. A dramatic looking tobacco ax and a double brass sweat strapper (for horses) created more comment than expected as I walked around with them tucked under my arm. I even bought a few tools — nothing great mind you, but some unusual pieces needing work. With my new outlook I had time to pick up some kitchen hangers for Doris.

We had detoured to Brimfield en route to my daughter's, and the plan was to make a short pit stop and push on for dinner in Boston. I enjoyed myself so much, between socializing and buying, that I made three trips back to the car and stayed four hours. They were probably the most relaxing four hours in a flea market I ever had.

Now, I'm not proposing that anyone try to build a collection with this browsing technique. There is no question that the good stuff goes early, and if you want it you have to get up in the dark and scramble. I'm merely admitting to a style of antiquing that I now consider to have merit. It's true that because of the enormity of Brimfield anything is possible, and if I had tried this at a smaller market I might have completely bombed out. However, that afternoon taught me something. Besides the thrill of the hunt, the satisfaction of possession, and the financial rewards of good buying, antiquing also offers the therapy of browsing.

Author's Note: As this article was written in 1986, there have been changes (mostly additions) to the Brimfield market openings. Check schedules in the *Maine Antique Digest.*

**"This is a rare set of Chelor match planes. One is genuine. The other is a genuine fake. I don't know which is which!"**

# 20

## A RARE DOUBLE COPING PLANE (1995)

Just when you have a handle on a topic, like wooden planemaking, something usually comes along that knocks a few of your well-formed theories into a cocked hat. Normally, an irregularity in planemaking occurs with a homemade plane. Here the unexplained can be resolved by merely writing off the maker as unknowledgeable, incompetent or just a kook. But when the weirdness occurs in a well-crafted, factory-made plane, you have to scratch your head.

Such a situation happened to me recently. I received a plane from my son in Maine that had both of us puzzled. At first glance it looked like a double coping plane. Looking closer, you might call it a sill plane. Looking even closer, you would hesitate to call it either. After searching the literature and making a few phone calls, I homed in on the answer. But first, the plane's description.

Its most perplexing characteristic was that it was made from *one piece of wood* (beech). See the photo. All the double coping planes I have seen were made from two pieces — the stock and the grip. In most cases these were put together perpendicular to each other, and in a few rarer cases at an angle around 60 degrees. Almost all double coping planes have their *grips fence the work*. This one does not.

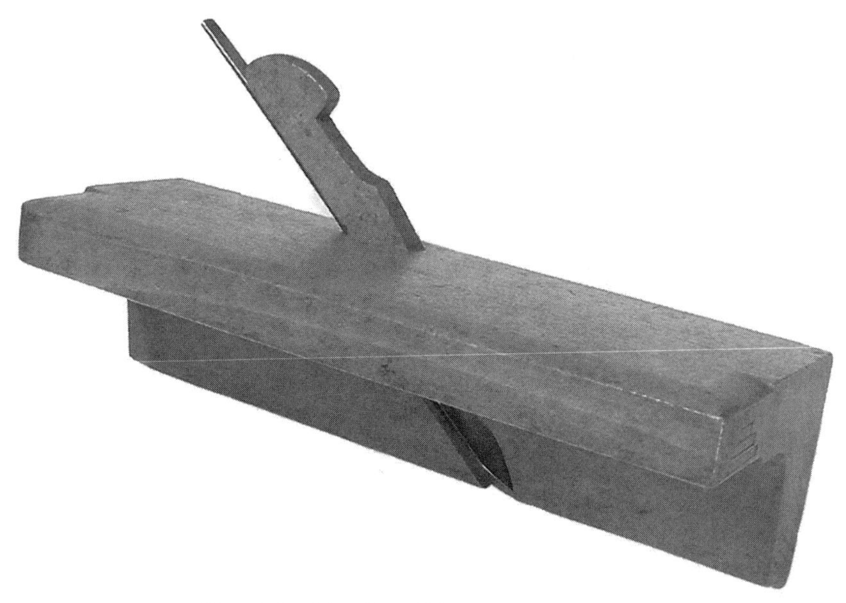

**Double Coping Plane, P. Sargent**

If you look at the body from the front view (see the sketch), you can see three more peculiarities: the body cross-section is *tapered*, the wedge and the iron are *tilted* on an angle, and this plane exits the chips on the same side that the grip is on, contrary to the standard double coping plane. If it were not for the fact that the profile is 1/2" , you might mistake it for a large sill plane. However, the drip cut for a sill plane is generally less than 1/4" wide. Also, all the sill planes I have seen have their wedges "open" on one side, probably because they are homemade and it was easier to make them that way. The plane in question has its wedge captured on both sides, and it is signed: *P. Sargent / Concord / N.H.*

Here's my feeling on why this plane is different from the double coping planes that we all know:

1. In Ken Roberts' book *Wooden Planes in 19th Century America*, a plane similar to this one is shown on page 258. Roberts calls it 18th century. It carries no maker's mark. Since getting my plane, I have talked to many of my dealer friends in an effort to get another, but most of them never even knew such a plane existed. Bill Gustafson and Roger

Smith were aware of these peculiar planes, and Roger had one that was unmarked and felt to be 18th century. It's very likely that Sargent copied the one-piece design from this earlier style. The obvious reason for the two-piece design was to save wood. Maybe Sargent had plenty of wood and didn't care about this factor.

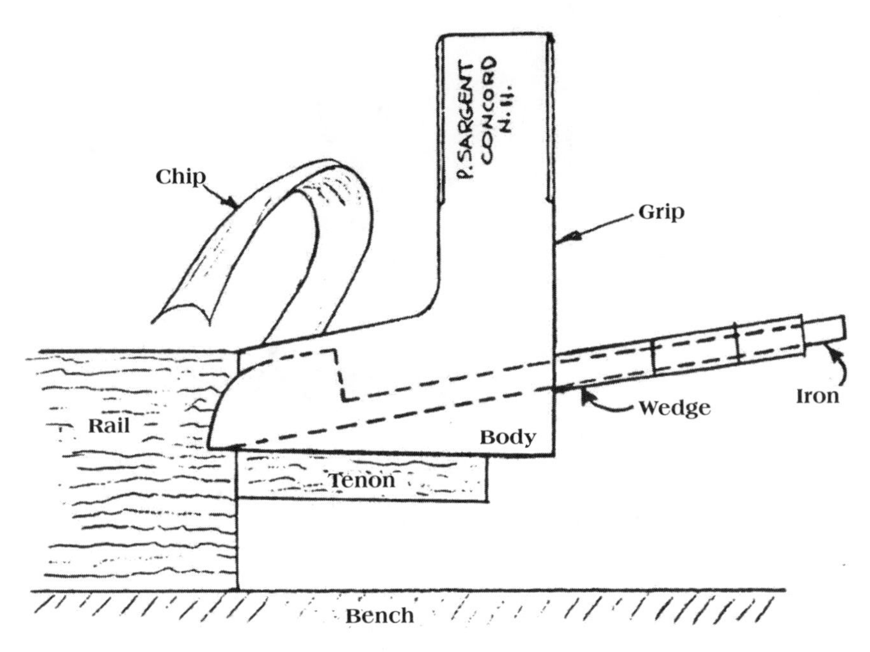


**Front View: Double Coping Plane in Working Position.**

2. The tapered body was produced to maintain a minimum wall thickness between the wedge and the right side of the body. It could have been untapered and wider, but that would have made it more difficult for chip exiting, and given it a less professional look.

3. The wedge and iron are tilted to prevent an "open" side to the wedge. A real planemaker would never allow the wedge to be anything but captured on both sides. (He also would not eat quiche.) This tilted characteristic is seen in French sash casement planes where the profile is similar to this plane. There are other ways that this could have been done, but this badger plane style seems to fit the bill.

4. The chips exit to the right, or up when the plane is laying on its left side, as in the sketch. In this position the left side is riding on the work and the chips cannot exit anywhere except the right side, the same side as the grip.

I'm sure everyone will sleep better tonight — now that this earth-shaking mystery is solved.

**"But everybody else gives a senior citizen's discount!"**

# 21

## TOOL WOODS
## (1993)

One cold morning at Shupp's Grove, many years ago, I came across a grimy plow plane. "How much?" I asked. The owner said he was looking for $40, "but with all that black paint on it," he would take $30. Turns out that there was no black paint at all. The plow was ebony! I've had similar windfalls with tools of boxwood, rosewood, apple, and other premium woods. It pays to know your woods, not only for value, but for the satisfaction of being able to completely identify a tool.

There are many wood identification books on the market, but few supply what the tool collector needs. Hoadley's *Identifying Wood* (Taunton Press), is one of the best, but requires time and effort to learn the wood technologist's language. We don't need to identify all the world's woods, just the twenty or so that were used professionally in tool making. This article tries to get through these woods with minimum buzzwords.

The two parts of the wood that make up **grain** (as seen by the naked eye) are the **pores** and the **rays**. Figure 1 identifies these as they appear in the various sections of the log.

Pores are the openings in the tiny tubes running up the tree that show up as holes when the tree is sawn across the trunk (**cross section**). The tree's **annual rings** result from having more, or larger, pores at the start of the growing season. If the pores are readily visible with the naked eye, the wood is termed **open grain**. If 5X magnification is needed, the wood is called **tight** or **close grain**.

The pores appear differently when the log is sawn lengthwise. They are now tiny grooves, such as you would get by cutting a bunch of straws lengthwise. In antique tools, these may be filled with grime, making them appear darker. If the cut is through the center of the tree (**radial section**), the annual rings appear as parallel lines. If the cut is at right angles to the radial section (**flat** or **tangential section**), the rings "wander" as in a contour map. See Fig. 1.

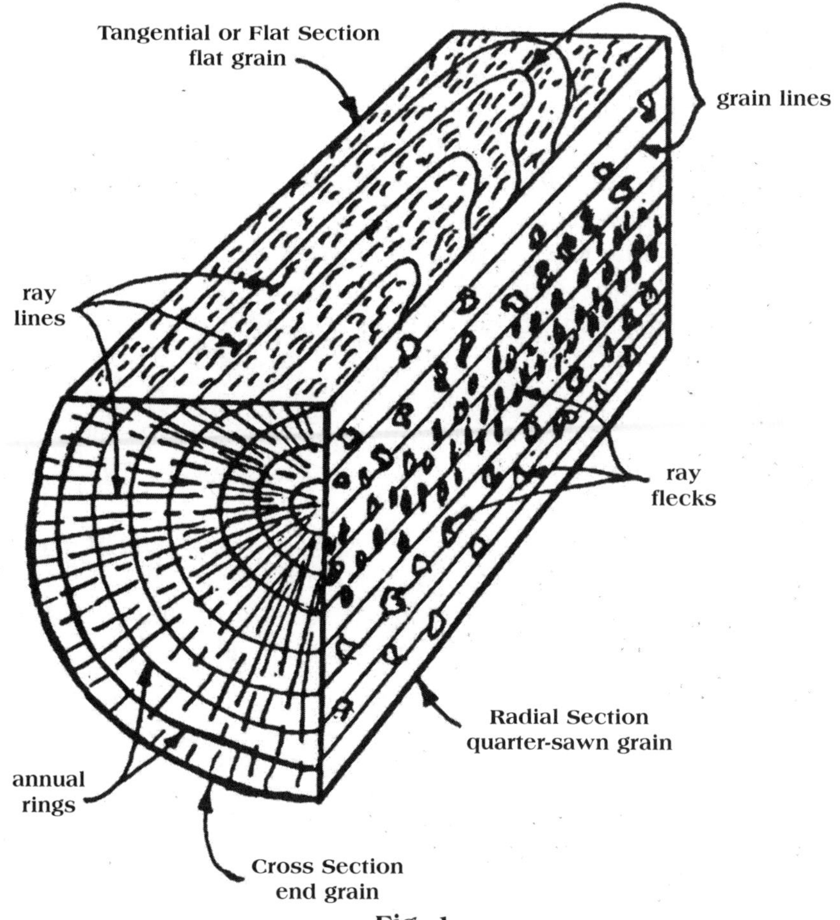


Fig. 1

The rays appear solid and flattened, and run outward from the center of the tree. In the cross section, they are seen as thin lines running from the core to the bark. In the radial section, they become irregular flecks, and in the flat section they are tiny straight lines. The rays are an important identification feature and usually need 5X magnification.

Two last definitions: the **sapwood** is a ring of wood next to the bark. It is usually much lighter in color than the remaining **heartwood**.

I believe that with just these terms you can identify the 20 or so common tool woods. I've found others: elm, sycamore, honey locust, teak, wenge, cormier, luan, cocobolo, satinwood, moradillo, etc., but they are insignificant in tool usage.

The clearest view of the pores and rays requires slicing the wood with a sharp razor. Not likely any of us would ever do this to a tool, unless it could be done on a hidden part. Cleaning the surface with #0000 steelwool will have to suffice. This will also help in determining the true color, as most tools have an aged surface (patina) that deepens their natural color.

Here are the woods:

**BOXWOOD**, European and Turkish

*(current substitutes are: Caribbean and Indonesian)*

Almost every tool collector is familiar with the hard homogeneous grain of boxwood rules. Molding plane wear strips, plow planes and miniatures also use boxwood. When this light yellow to buff wood patinates and darkens, it might be mistaken for maple. Maple's end grain under 5X magnification has very distinct ray lines, while boxwood's rays are so thin and close together that they could be missed even under magnification. Apple, particularly its sapwood, is occasionally taken for boxwood; but it is much grainier and has a pinkish-brown hue (as opposed to the yellowish cast of boxwood).

**MAPLE**, Sugar *(also called Rock or Hard)*

A sandy-colored wood with tight grain. Rays in the flat section are thin lines about 1/64" long. They show as flecks in the radial section. Maple can be found in primitive braces, chisel and other handles, log rules, cooper's howels and crozes. The figured **birdeye** and **tiger** grains are seen sometimes in measuring tools. Signed planes in maple are rare.

**BEECH**, American

This is the most commonly used tool wood, particularly in planes. It is tan in color, but can patinate to a deep walnut. The key to beech is its rays: prominent flecks in the radial section, and thin lines in the flat section (which can go over 1/16" long). The fact that the flat section rays are easily visible to the naked eye helps differentiate beech from birch and maple.

**BIRCH**, Yellow

Used mostly in early New England planes, it is sometimes confused with beech and maple. It is grainier than either, the flat section showing open pores up to 1/2" long, (usually darkened with grime). Magnification is needed to see the rays in any section. At 5X they show in the cross section as narrower than the pores. (The rays in maple are the same size as the pores, and in beech they are considerably wider than the pores).

**APPLE**

Used in planes, an occasional primitive brace, and non-impact handles, particularly saw handles. It has very tight grain, and shows no rays to the naked eye. Its heartwood is pinkish-brown; its sapwood much lighter.

**CHERRY**, Black

Primarily used in levels and non-impact handles, it is grainier than apple. Radial sections show pronounced ray flecks, but none are seen in apple. Cherry's sapwood is light tan, and a stripe of it is generally seen in levels.

**HORNBEAM**, European

A wood of yellowish-tan cast, common in central European tools, particularly German and Austrian planes and braces. It has wide rays, about the width of those in oak. They show as flecks sometimes 1/4" wide by an inch, long. You'll have to look closely, as the color of the rays is almost the same as the base wood.

**HICKORY**, various

Used almost exclusively in impact handles (axes, hammers, etc.). I do own a hickory plane and a brace, but these are exceptions. Pores are large in diameter and very long in the lengthwise sections (up to 3"). No rays are visible to the naked eye, which differentiates it from oak. The sapwood is buff and the heartwood light to medium brown.

**ASH**, various

Not many tools use ash; a plane or two, Dutch and English braces, and some handles. Ash has large pores like hickory and oak, but no rays are visible to the eye (unlike oak). The heartwood is very light tan. The subtle difference between ash and hickory (besides color), is in the pores. In ash they are generally under 1/2" long, while in hickory they are over 1/2". Another difference can be seen in the end grain. Ash has a tight cluster of large pores (2 or 3 deep), right at the ring line, while hickory has the pores more distributed between ring lines.

**OAK**, Red and White

The common red and white oaks are rarely used in any but homemade tools. They have large pores, long rays in the flat section (up to 1" long), and almost a garish ray fleck pattern when quarter-sawn in the radial section.

**OAK**, Live

Live oak is much heavier and darker brown than the common oaks, and has a more twisted grain. Its pores are smaller, but its rays are thicker and more pronounced. It was used mostly for bench planes. It is on the borderline of sinking; most of the time it will sink slowly.

**OAK**, Cork

Growing mostly in Spain and Portugal, this tree's bark is harvested for cork. Many of the long shouldered rabbet planes and plow planes from this area are of this wood, as are hand adze handles. It is very similar to our live oak, except it is lighter brown and doesn't sink.

**OAK**, English

Also called brown oak (because of its brown color, naturally). It sometimes has a striped or figured look.

**OAK**, Japanese

Lighter in color than our live oak, with straight grain and shorter, thinner rays. It is used in Japanese and Chinese planes.

**WALNUT**, Black

Except for some infills of English planes, a few measuring and homemade tools, not many other tools are made of this wood. It is straight-grained and brown in color, without any reddish cast. Although color is the best means of separating walnut from mahogany, end grain, under 5X magnification will help. Walnut's rays are very hard to see, and it has more pores than mahogany, mainly due to walnut's pores diminishing in size as they move outward from the annual ring. This produces the telltale "shaded" look to the grain line in the flat section.

**MAHOGANY**, Central American *(various species)* Commonly called Honduras Mahogany, from the former principle source, these look-alikes are light reddish-brown with well defined pores in all sections. A ribboned appearance is common in mahogany, caused by changes in grain direction in adjacent areas. These woods are not as heavy as Cuban mahogany or the rosewoods, nor do they have the swirling dark stripes of the latter. Rays are obvious under 5X magnification, in contrast to walnut and rosewood. Mahogany is used in levels, measuring tools, and English plane infills.

**MAHOGANY**, Cuban

This wood is no longer available, but can be found in antique levels. It is considerably heavier than the Central American mahoganies (bordering on sinking), and is tighter-grained and much darker.

**ROSEWOOD**, East Indian *(also called Indian)*

One of the premier tool woods. It has a medium brown to purplish-brown color with dark brown (almost black) stripes. Pores can easily be seen in all sections under 5X magnification, but not rays. It was used for plane handles, levels, measuring tools, premier planes and braces.

**ROSEWOOD**, Brazilian

This more dramatically grained rosewood is orangey-brown to medium brown with swirling jet black stripes. It was used similar to Indian rosewood. The difference between Brazilian and Indian is subtle when color is not a strong enough clue. Brazilian is heavier, more aromatic when abraded, and has tighter grain (sparser pores). Unfortunately these three characteristics are not easy to evaluate in the finished tool. If you can't get a good look at the end grain, you may have to accept the fact that you can only identify it as a rosewood, nothing more.

**ROSEWOOD**, Honduras

A much lighter colored pinkish-brown to orangey-brown with less figure and straighter grain than the rosewoods above. Used in premier planes and levels. It is generally heavy enough to sink.

**LIGNUM VITAE**

Common in Sheffield brace heads, it was also used in ship's planes, mallets and in the boxing strips of planes from the Philadelphia area. The color varies (many times in the same piece) from olive-brown to reddish-brown with yellowish-brown stripes. It generally becomes very dark with age. Its yellowish-tan sapwood may form part of a brace or plane, etc. The grain is very tight, and is distinctly interlocked (reversing). Pores can just about be seen at 5X magnification, but not rays. A dusty (some say spicy) odor can be detected, even without scuffing. It sinks like a rock.

**EBONY**, Ceylon *(now called Sri Lanka)*

This basically black ebony has a light gray sapwood. It was used for braces (Ultimatums), plow planes, bow drills, ship's planes, infills for English planes, handles and measuring tools. The pores are harder to pick out than the rosewoods; the rays are almost undetectable, even under 5X magnification. Ceylon is the heaviest of the ebonys; it sinks quickly.

**EBONY**, Macassar

A dark brown ebony with medium brown stripes, and a buff-colored sapwood. It was used similar to Ceylon. Although not as dense as Ceylon, it still sinks.

**EBONY**, African (various species)

Some species have black heartwood, others a black and brown striped heartwood, still others black with grayish-brown streaks. All have light colored sapwood, and all sink. Ebony is another group of species that might be hard to differentiate. Unfortunately, wood can vary drastically (even within a species), based upon growing conditions and locale. To get down to the nitty-gritty of which solid black ebony is which, you will need more buzzwords and higher magnification. We'll let that go for another time.

The best way to learn these tool woods is to examine samples large enough to see all three sections. Some may be available from commercial sources, but some are no longer found, except in old tools. I am making up sample wood kits, just for tool collectors. Come to the April meeting and see the tool woods on display, most in samples, all in tools.

# 22

## THE TOOL DUNGEON
## (1991)

In my first days of tool collecting, many of the tools were English. Pieces from the U.K. were as much sought after as those from this country. Most of the coopers' tools were English or Scottish, and no one really cared where they were from. Molding planes were molding planes, and whether they were Greenfield or Norwich they sold for $4.00 ($5.00 to $9.00 if they were wide). As a collector, you are probably tired of hearing how cheap things were in the "good-ole-days." And you might rightly respond that every collectible went through that period. True! But I'd like to use this background to set the tone for a type of sale that was held in those days that was exciting and profitable for both the buyer and the seller.

In the early 1970's England was ripe for U.S. tool dealers that wanted to buy in bulk. English tools were plentiful, and oddly enough, there were very few English tool collectors, in comparison to those in the States. So it was with great interest that U.S. tool dealers were invited into the inner sanctum of English commerce, and even into English countryhouses. Some of these U.S. dealers resold the pieces at auction, others at retail shops; a few started mail order catalogs that combined English and American tools. But one man devised a plan to market these tools that was to be the most exciting.

Win Carter was one of the grand old gentlemen of the tool business, and was highly respected, both in this country and in England. Carter Antiques in Portsmouth, N. H. (which is still run by Scotty Carter, his wife) is on a quaint waterfront street in a wonderful old brick building overlooking the Piscataqua River, separating Maine from New Hampshire. The main retail area is on the first floor — great antiques, Americana, decoys, etc. — with the bulk of the tools in the basement.

In order to get to the basement you had to wind your way down a steep, spiral staircase (as if you were going into a medieval dungeon). At the bottom was a creaky door that provided entry into what to me, at the time, was the greatest array of tools for sale anywhere in the country. It was breathtaking because Win was an excellent buyer, and did not believe in junk. His stuff was all good looking and generally in full working order.

Now comes the mouthwatering part. Exactly at the stroke of 9:00, Win would announce to the 12 to 15 invitees waiting in line, "Gentlemen, it's time." It was almost as if you were at the Indianapolis Speedway on Memorial Day. The door at the top of the staircase would open and everyone would start down in a single file. The narrow stairs precluded anyone getting out of position. But once at the bottom and through the door to the tool room, most of us dropped our "cool" and went nuts! Everything was laid out neatly and in order: planes in the racks — each shelf a different price — braces in one area, measuring instruments on tables, cooper's tools in the back, tiny sparklers in cabinets, chisels in the center, saws on the wall, and toolboxes on the floor. What a sight!

Only business propriety prevents me from saying how much was sold in those first few minutes. The biggest problem was to decide quickly enough whether you wanted an item. There was no time to inspect, as precious seconds would be wasted and the great piece laying a foot away would not be there a minute or two later. The rule of etiquette of these 12 to 15 people was that if you put it in your box, you bought it — no putting back at the end. For the most part, this rule and other politeness was diligently followed. Looking back, however, I can remember one dealer grabbing five out of seven Ultimatums. The reason he didn't take all seven was that he couldn't get anymore under his arms. In another instance, one fellow just wiped all the miniatures off the shelf with one swoop of his arm. We appealed to Win that although there was nothing in the "rules" to prohibit this, the majority would like it stopped. I don't recall it happening again.

You might ask, why the frenzied buying, particularly from knowledgeable dealers and collectors. The answer was simple: great stuff at very reasonable prices. Win saw to it that you didn't have to waste time looking at the price tag. If you really liked the piece, or felt that it had good resale potential, you could almost always be assured that the price was right.

The sale would last only an hour or so, and the remainder of at least a thousand tools would then be offered to the general public. This is not to say that the only time I visited Carter's was on Dealer Day. He constantly got stuff in from the locals, and I never missed stopping there on my way to Maine.

You too can experience some of these adventures. I can't guarantee the price structure, as things never stay the same economically, and the horn of plenty is tough to fill with tools these days. But Scotty Carter still goes to England, and still brings back some great pieces, and still has an open shop and an occasional Dealer Day. I stop there whenever I can. It brings back the nostalgia of the winding stairs and the cry, "Gentlemen, it's time."

# 23

## ROT RESTORATION
### (1994)

In restoration work one of the nastiest things to work with is rot. It sometimes becomes so frustrating that the repair just can't be made. In recent years, I've taken this as a challenge, and devised all kinds of techniques to try to lick the problem. In most cases, the standard methods do work, but every now and then you must become a little creative.

Small rot areas can most often be "solidified" with commercial two-part marine epoxies such as *GIT-ROT* or other brands. If there is no break in the surface to apply these fillers, then they can be shot into the rot area via drill holes and a hypodermic type needle very much like the ones used to introduce glue under existing veneer. The problem with this is that if you apply it wrong, or the configuration is hidden from view and not as you anticipated, then you have a mess to remove when it fails. Sometimes it's not worth the gamble and you are better off going directly to the "cut-away" method.

This technique is exactly what it sounds like: the affected area is literally cut away and new matching wood put in its place. Woodworkers have been doing this for quite some time, as I have found tools from the 18th century with "dutchmen" that look like they were put in hundreds of years ago. Needless to say, you have to be a real woodworker to put a clean dutchman in a rot area and have it look good. But more problemsome than that is the fear that when you start to clean out the affected area it just keeps growing. Here's where the frustration sets in. After you have almost half of the entire piece cut away and there is still not much solid wood showing up, you realize that you have just blown the project. At this point hindsight is terrific, "Why didn't I just leave it alone?"

Well there is another way, one that isn't as drastic as "cut-away" and actually is easier. Most rot is under the surface, and a thin layer of solid wood generally covers the punky area. When this is the case you can try the "layback" technique. Slit the rot area with the grain and layback the pieces that cover the area. If you are careful (and lucky) you will have two solid pieces that will later come back into their original positions. See Fig. 1.

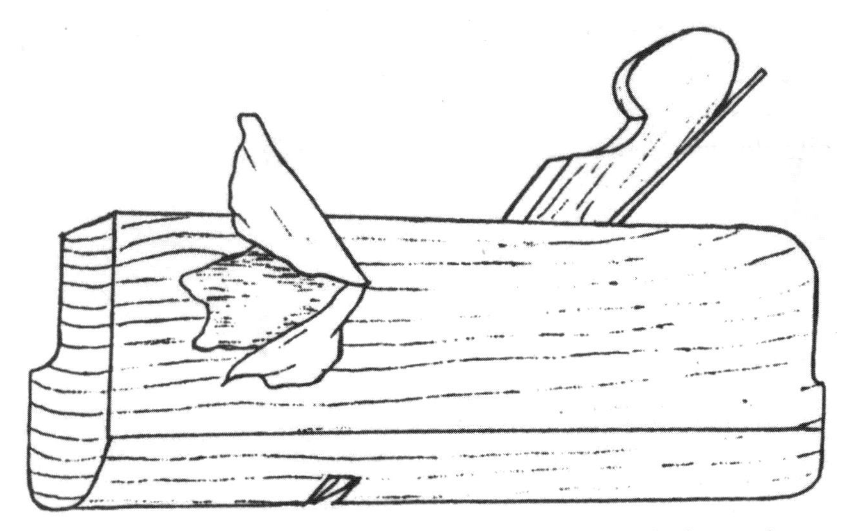

**Fig. 1. Rot area slit longitudinally, and external pieces bent back exposing rot.**

Lay aside the "cover" pieces and dig out the rot. This may end up quite surprising. As in Figure 2, a spot that originally seemed no bigger than a thumbnail turned out to be $2\frac{1}{4}$" by $2\frac{1}{4}$" by $\frac{3}{8}$" deep! Care must be taken not to disturb

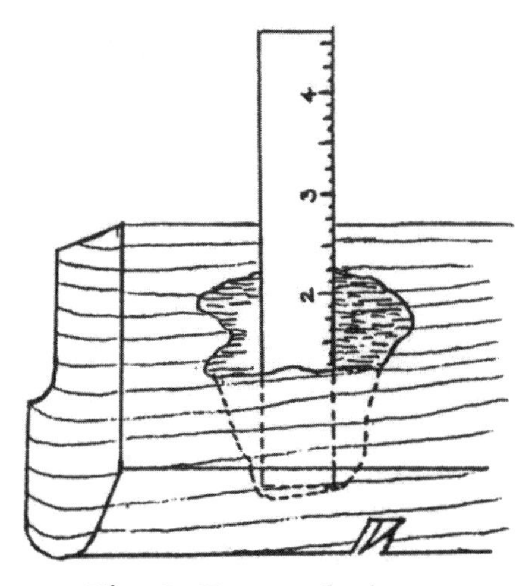


**Fig. 2. External pieces removed and saved. Rot removed (over 1" down in pocket and 3/8" deep); overall rot area: 2 1/4" x 2 1/4" x 3/8".**

any outer surface area, or a gap will occur when you replace the cover pieces. If you're not as lucky as I was, you may have to cut extra cover pieces to get at areas you never dreamed were rotten. At any rate, it's all "do-able" if you have the patience.

Now you can fill with just about any epoxy that is not too viscous, as you need it to flow into all the nooks and crannies. The marine epoxies are probably best here, because they have a penetrating capillary-flow action. Before the epoxy sets, you must put the cover pieces back in place. You will probably find that you have too much epoxy and some will have to be squeezed out with the cover pieces. If you do it right, it is hard to tell what happened. See Fig. 3.

I'm sure the most common reaction of anyone reading this article is, "Is he kidding?" I know I just described a lot of work without a good probability of complete success. But aren't you tired of making excuses for rotted crown molders or ending up practically giving them away?

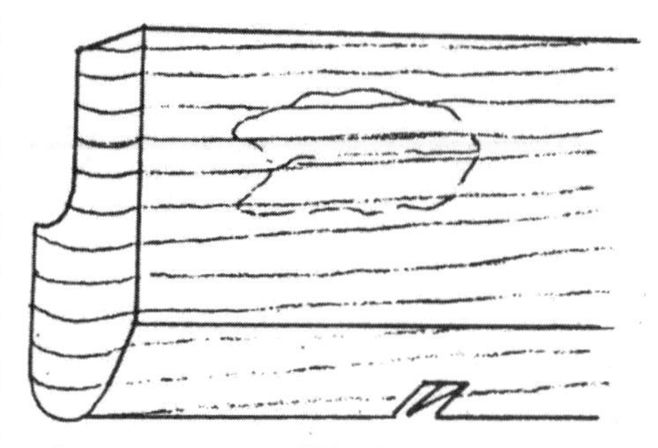

**Fig. 3. Epoxy filled and external pieces put back in place.**

# 24

## REMOVING PLANE WEDGES
## (1996)

The wooden plane user of years ago was primarily interested in getting the wedge out of the plane for resetting or resharpening. He didn't always have a vise or the right size mallet handy in order to achieve flawless removal. I'm not sure that he cared terribly about any nicks or dents to the plane that occurred during this process, and he was probably willing to take the risk of an occasional split finial. He did have the advantage that the wedges were in and out of the planes on a regular basis, and were rarely "frozen" as we sometimes find them today. We collectors care a lot about deformity and, consequently, our removal techniques might differ from those of craftsmen of yesteryear.

In the March 1996 *Chronicle*, Jim Gauntlett asks the provocative question: "Are the rounded ends on molding plane wedges (finials) designed for any reason *other* than wedge removal?" I think not. I think that the finial design is basically functional, even though it was used as a sort of signature shape by each maker. Planemakers knew that if the plane was stored and used properly, and the strike on the finial was done at the right angle and momentum, very little damage would be done. As such, Jim gives a removal technique that includes striking the finial. However, in a subsequent issue (June 1996) Charles R. Wright disagrees with this technique and points out that there are many molding planes with their finials partially or completely split away from being hit with a mallet. I certainly can attest to that fact, even though I believe it was through carelessness. Charles recommends one solid blow to the back of the plane. But does this work all the time? I have restored hundreds of planes and can report that many of the various techniques work *most* of the time, but not without occasional problems. There is, however, a technique that works *all* of the time, and 1) does little or no damage to the plane, 2) is relatively quick, 3) doesn't require much skill, and 4) differentiates between bench plane wedges and molding plane wedges.

Here it is for your consideration:

### Molding Planes

If you put the wedge in a vise, as shown in Figure 1, and tap the heel of the plane, the wedge will loosen easily. Other techniques hold the plane in the vise (or even in your hand) and tap the finial, but that could lead to "abusive tapping" with the resultant split and deformed finials that we have all found. Here lies the beauty of the technique shown in Figure 1: it's almost impossible to abuse the plane, particularly if you use a mallet rather than a hammer. However, it's important that the mallet be hard enough to shock the wedge. Dampening the blow too much with a rubber head won't get the job done.

### Bench Planes

Here, many of the existing techniques work well. Take for instance a smoother. Striking it on the heel, while it lays flat on the bench against a stop, usually is successful. On jacks and fore planes, hitting the strike button (located forward of the throat on the top side) normally will loosen all but a really frozen wedge. If there is no strike button, you will be taking a chance of denting the plane's body if you don't use a protective block of wood at the position where the button would normally be. Unfortunately this reduces the shock value of the blow, and if you are dealing with a long jointer (24" or over), you need all the jolt that you can get. However, I have planes that you could hit with a trip hammer (at this position), and not loosen the wedge. Many early crowns without strike buttons have their top surface completely torn up from unsuccessful blows at this location. So, how then?

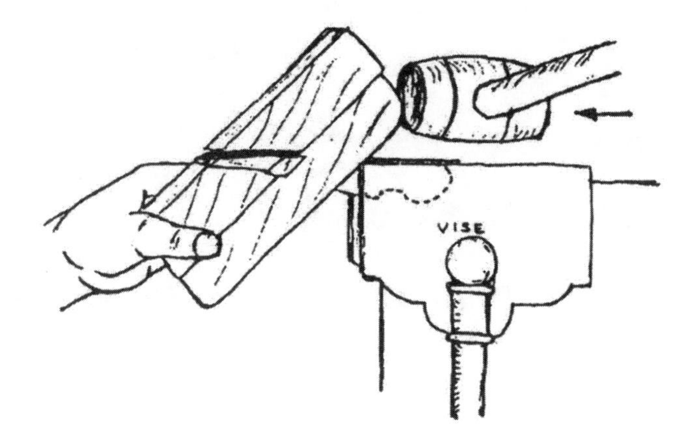


**Fig. 1**

Gentleness and patience should guide your first try. Tap the *side* of the wedge (one side, then the other) until a slight looseness is perceived. Then wiggle the wedge back and forth and *upward.* Repeat the tapping if necessary. I have rarely had a wedge that couldn't be loosened in this manner. But, when all else failed, I would put the wedge into a vise, similar to Figure 1, and hit the heel of the plane with a heavy mallet. This never failed!

Where tapered irons are present (either in bench or molding planes) tapping the iron deeper into the plane, to break any friction between the wedge and the iron, sometimes helps. If the wedge is really swollen against the body, even this will not loosen it, and you will have to proceed further as above. If the iron isn't tapered, you might make it worse by driving it deeper.

I don't recommend trying to remove a frozen wedge without a vise. But if you have to, remember patience is the byword. Shock and vibration will eventually loosen most anything. The trick is to apply them with care.

# 25

## FROM JACK PLANE TO "SNAKE PLANE" (1997)

*Published by the National Wood Carvers Association.*

I remember when I was in the seventh grade, one of our first projects in Wood Shop was to take a rough board, saw it to a specific size and then hand plane it flat and square. I kept making mistakes and had to take away wood to correct the problem — the piece kept getting smaller and smaller. It was a nightmare! The other boys didn't fare much better.

Finally, with a smile on his face, the teacher let us out of our misery by telling us that although that exercise looked simple, it took an apprentice quite some time before he was able to master it.

In my future dealings with woodworking and carving, I stayed away from such frustration by using power jointers, thickness planers and sanders. But now in my retirement, I constantly look for challenges, the type that no one knows about and which can be quickly abandoned if it goes the wrong way.

Such a project was my "snake plane" — a carving that was to be artistic, geometrically complex, and functional. Happily, it was a success and I have a unique piece to show for my effort.

Since early times, there has been an occasional piece that had a beautiful look besides being functional. In the 1700's it was not uncommon for European planes to be adorned with low relief carving. It is not known whether the planemakers did the carving or gave the job to more experienced carvers. Some of these planes still survive and are treasured in museums and private collections.

There are woodworkers today who have taken on the task of making a plane, some just to prove their skills, others to add to their collections. (Antique tool collecting is getting to be a serious hobby throughout the world.) The difficulty of these projects lies in the precise cuts needed to maintain the blade angle, minimal mouth opening, and snug wedge fit. The work is more on the order of precision joinery than artistic carving. Nevertheless, most of it can only be done with chisels.

In looking back at pictures of ornate planes, I found that almost all of the plane bodies were made first and then the front knobs and rear handles fit separately into the bodies. This was the logical way to produce planes economically, rather than carving everything from one piece. However, my design, with carvings blocking the free action of a hand plane, forced the squaring of those surfaces with chisels! The thought of flattening and squaring a block of wood with a chisel was frightening to me as the dimensional tolerances were very close and I thought about that seventh grade debacle.

When I was confident I could finish the project, I added chip carving, scroll work, outline cuts, and ivory fangs. But what was most satisfying was that the original design was achieved - a snake being both the front grip and the rear handle, in addition to it being integral to the body. I believe this is a first.

The carving is 13" by 6" by 4" of light mahogany. The plane is functional, cutting a shaving as fine as .0015" thick — about $^{1}/_{4}$ the size of a human hair.

"Your tools go or I go!" "I'm waiting!" "I'm thinking!"

# 26

## THE GOOD OLE DAYS
## (1989)

Have you ever yearned for the days when you eagerly bought marking gauges, squares and beat-up bench planes? If you spent over $5 for anything, 'twas close to traumatic. But didn't you have a lot more fun than the more sophisticated collecting of today?

Now-a-days a beginner starts right out with all kinds of books and catalogs, and isn't very interested in "starter" tools. He bids right along with everybody else on rosewood plowplanes and ivory rules. As an auctioneer I suppose I should be cheering this, but as a collector I feel somewhat jealous. Where is his apprenticeship? Where is his time served banging around garage sales and flea markets, learning the hard way? I really believe the guy is missing a lot of fun.

When I started, it didn't hurt too much to learn that the plane you just bought had an improper wedge — you had only paid $3.50 for it anyway. But when you buy a complete fake for some pretty decent bucks, it hurts bad. So the beginner today has to get serious from the start, and there goes most of the fun.

Graduating to the ranks of the advanced collector is no great thrill either. I find myself ignoring almost all the tools shown in shops and fleas because I can tell very quickly that they are already in my collection, and almost all are of the common variety anyway. So you could go an entire day at Lambertville/New Hope, or worse yet, an entire day at Adamstown, with very little to show for it. Oh sure, there will be the day you catch that big one. But those days are few and far between. Isn't this whole plightful affair the natural evolution of things? Doesn't everything start off primitive and get sophisticated as it grows up? Alas, it's true; but wasn't it more fun swimming in the "ole deep hole" than it is today in the heated YMCA pool? I crave the "good ole days" when buying a $2 square was real fun, particularly when someone told you that the handle was *rosewood*!

How then can some of us who have reached this place in collecting go backwards again? How can we once more get to enjoy collecting? Give our collections to charity and start over? Not likely. Box everything and begin again? Most collections are in boxes right now anyhow. So what then?

Ever see the bumper sticker that reads: TAKE A BOY FISHING? Fishermen have gone through this exact phenomenon. Catching sunfish on pin hooks and worms was great fun and you never lacked for fish. But as you progressed along, your equipment and your goals became more sophisticated than you might have really desired. Pretty soon you had all the right knowledge and tangible assets, but not too many fish. What to do? Live vicariously! Take a boy fishing and start over. No one would really figure out that you were having more fun than the boy.

Taking a boy out "tooling" to kindle his interest in manual arts, fixing around the house, collecting, or just to generate pride in his heritage is a notable cause all by itself. And if you happen to have more fun than he does while doing it, who says that's a crime?

# 27

## A REAL LEMON
## (1993)

If anyone wanted to spend the time to analyze all the antique tools that were professionally produced, they might come up with a paradox something like this: the more ineffective a thing was, the more valuable it is today. Sure, that's an oversimplification, but the basis of this premise is rarity. If it's near useless, even those who were gullible enough to fall for the outrageous claims of the maker will eventually badmouth the thing out of existence. Although rarity is not the only criterion for value, it is an important one.

So it was when I was given a humble looking wooden smooth plane to restore. It had a piece of the sole cut out just forward of the mouth. This is a common malady of planes repaired with sole inserts, as shrinkage sometimes causes the insert to fall out. So I looked at the nose to see if the maker was valuable enough to warrant restoration, but found no mark at all. If I was dealing with a beginner-collector, I would have told him to save the wedge and iron and throw the body away. (I know some readers will cringe just thinking about throwing anything away.) But this was a collector who knew what he was doing, so I finally asked, "O.K., what's the secret here?" The "secret" was that this plane broke the rule of "maker's marks are always on the nose." On the heel was stamped: L. C. Ashley/Patented Feb/1856.

Who was Ashley, and what in the world was so special about a sole insert? At this point the owner of the plane whipped out the patent papers which described the plane in glorious detail, professing that it would cure everything from torn grain to tennis elbow. But the patent did solve the mystery of the cut-away sole. In part of that opening went an iron sole insert with a long flange that attached to a tongue-like wooden piece in the throat. See Fig. 1.

**Fig. 1 As Designed**

The inventor lauded his geometric perfection of all angles, etc., stating that the plane would maintain a perfect mouth opening even as the stock wore away. But looking at the plane. I couldn't see what he was referring to, because there was no tongue-like piece to provide any angular control. The throat was clean. See Fig. 2. Well almost clean. Closer examination showed an outline where the throat-piece used to be, and some hack marks that were made

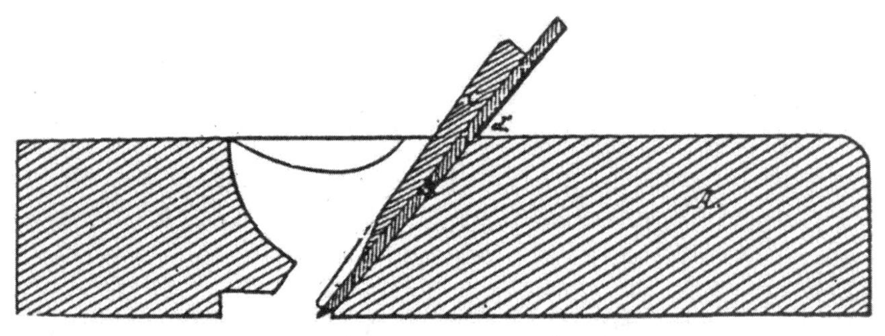

**Fig. 2 As Found**

during its removal. In addition, it was evident that the sole had been cut into to provide a seat for the replacement wooden insert. The obvious questions came quickly: why would anyone destroy such a "spectacular" idea, and why go through so much work to do it? I suppose in those days it was cheaper to fix something (no matter how time consuming) rather than buy new. But what was the problem to start with? Only two possibilities came to mind: the plane was dropped and the iron piece (most likely a casting) cracked and was scrapped. Not being able to get another, or not wanting to spend the money, the owner modified the sole with a wooden insert. Why then did he cut away the throat-piece? A more likely explanation was that the throat-piece was clogging the chips and making it very difficult to remove them. In short, it was a poor design.

Proudly I handed back the plane and the patent papers, and gave him my evaluation, "No need to spend money fixing up this lemon." However, the other guy's "calculator" must have been active while I was expounding my theory, as he was now honestly excited. He explained that if this plane was as bad as I said, there probably wouldn't be many around today, in any condition; and if I made it like the patent papers it might be quite rare, even though restored. Embarrassed, I could only respond, "I knew that."

So I restored it the way Mr. L. C. Ashley designed it, and sure enough the chips clogged and were tough to remove. As I was grumbling about putting out a product with out testing it, my wife reminded me that many of her household items are near worthless because they were never tried by the people who were to use them. Her favorite expression for such a lemon is, "This must have been designed by a man." What she really means is that it must have been designed by someone who was not a homemaker.

This prompts me to the following conclusion: the plane patented by L. C. Ashley, Patent No. 14436, must have been designed by someone who was not a woodworker. I wonder how many others are like that?

# 28

## THE CAPE COD CAPER
## (A GRAMPA TOOL STORY)
## (1993)

Each year we go to a different place for vacation. Don't ask me why. Many of those places have been great, and warranted a return visit, but she-who-must-be-obeyed likes to try something new each year. This is not to say that we don't visit the same area again, but never the same cottage or inn. Cape Cod has been her favorite spot for the past few years, and we always invite my daughter's family up, as they live nearby.

My function for these vacations has been mainly chauffeur, payer of bills, and reservation maker. I get to go fishing by myself occasionally, and hit the antique shops with the whole family. But I don't do much in the way of *adventurous* tool-hunting; and we all know that the hunt is the backbone of collecting.

As I sat on the porch, during our last vacation, overlooking a beautiful ocean vista, I felt a pang of restlessness. I should have been relaxed in that environment, but what was nagging at me was the unfullfilled need for a good tool hunt on the Cape. It seemed as if everyone always wanted to go somewhere else. I made up my mind that this was to be my year.

When my 8 year old grandson came bounding onto the porch tugging at me to take him fishing, an idea was born. I knew it was tough keeping any 8 year old occupied at the same thing for any length of time, and fishing is a tough activity when they aren't biting. But *what if* I had a secondary activity planned that would take over after the fishing interlude petered out? And *what if* my grandson could be convinced to look for toys, etc. in the various antique shops that we visit? Travel time over 10 or 15 minutes could be interspersed with ice cream and junk food. Although I considered the idea a work of art, I felt that my daughter might not agree, so I didn't bother to tell her all the boring details; only that we were going fishing and that we wouldn't be back for lunch. Both mother and daughter loved the plan. They now had time for uninterrupted shopping.

It was the only time I ever cursed the fish for biting so soon and so voraciously. But how many perch and bluegills can an 8 year old catch before opting for ice cream? Finally, we were on our way . . . tool-hunting at last. No one waiting in the car for me, no lunch to herd everyone together for, just plain adventure!

Now, tooling on the Cape is not what you could call lucrative. There are only three full fledged tool dealers and a couple of flea markets. Most of the shops with only a few tools are picked over pretty heavily. So what does that leave? The random treasure that we all seek.

A cap gun, a steamshovel and two ice creams later I sensed that I had pushed the caper to the limit, and had almost nothing to show for it. But it was still fun. The anticipation was the thing I told myself. So, we started back to the cottage. As fate would have it, one more shop got in our way.

The stuff in this shop looked ripe for a treasure, as everything was piled helter-skelter (uncharacteristic of the shops on Cape Cod). My grandson was pulling a repro tomahawk out of a pile when a bunch of things fell to the floor. As he was picking the items up to put them back (my daughter taught him good manners), he announced that there were "some tools here."

I knew it! I rushed in half expecting to be blinded by the glare of the Mother Lode. But my dream popped when I saw only rusty pliers and beat-up screwdrivers. But wait — an odd shaped screwdriver was laying amidst the clutter. Its handle had the look of a can of snuff. Even though the patina of this weird handle was very dark, you could still see the elaborate engraving and the telltale green oxide indicating brass.

Cleaned up, it proved to be a patented ratchet screwdriver, both beautiful and rare. It was the prize trophy of our "fishing trip." It only goes to show that even in these more sophisticated times of tool collecting, and even in a comparatively barren area for treasures, adventure still awaits us. How many other collectibles can this be said about?

**"Hey dad, that nice Mr. Wilson gave me these dandy baseball cards for those old wood planes in your glass case!"**

# 29

## HIDDEN SIMPLICITY
## (1996)

There are times when the complexity of a situation reaches a point where it appears as if only a genius or a space-age computer could handle it. It is times like these when I have felt that perhaps the brain of mere man, by itself, is not enough to function in our high-tech world. But something always drags me back in time to point out how yesterday's "mere man" was able to solve problems that today's sophisticated intelligentsia find formidable: sailing ships, pyramids, Stonehenge, and the like. Some of these techniques still impress our scientists. How did they do it centuries ago?

Most of the answers are known, or speculated at, and most make good sense. But every now and then, something comes along that piques our curiosity, sometimes to the point of embarrassment. We wonder how anyone without our elaborate education and equipment could do the things that they did. An example, although never thought of as anything except a common utilitarian item, is the barrel.

The concept of the barrel can be seen in drawings as far back as the early Egyptians. With their intelligence it is easy to understand how they progressed from hollowed-out tree sections to staves forced together with wooden hoops. However, these vessels were only tapered tubs and buckets and did not incorporate the "belly" of the later Roman barrels. The purpose of the belly is obvious to anyone who has ever rolled a barrel. A bellied barrel can be easily rolled and turned due to the small surface area contacting the ground. It does away with the conical bucket-type vessel that doesn't roll in a straight line. There are other advantages: additional strength provided by the arch effect, the ability to drive the hoops from both ends (a perfect cylinder without a belly would not allow the hoops to be driven), and the ease of tilting the barrel upright from its horizontal position.

But nothing is more puzzling than how this belly was accomplished, keeping in mind the two main criteria of a "wet" barrel: 1) it must not leak, and 2) it must hold a rather exact amount of liquid.

The skill of preventing the barrel from leaking requires an explanation that must be reserved for a more lengthy article. The subject of this article is: how could men without any education (many could not even sign their names) and without power tools of any kind, maintain an almost unbelievable accuracy relating to the volume of the barrel.

Kenneth Kilby, in his book *The Cooper and His Trade*, describes a simple tool that he calls diagonals. Most are merely two pointed sticks bolted together at their ends so as to pivot. They look exactly like a pair of primitive dividers. See Fig. 1 . But this is where the similarity ends. The tool (it

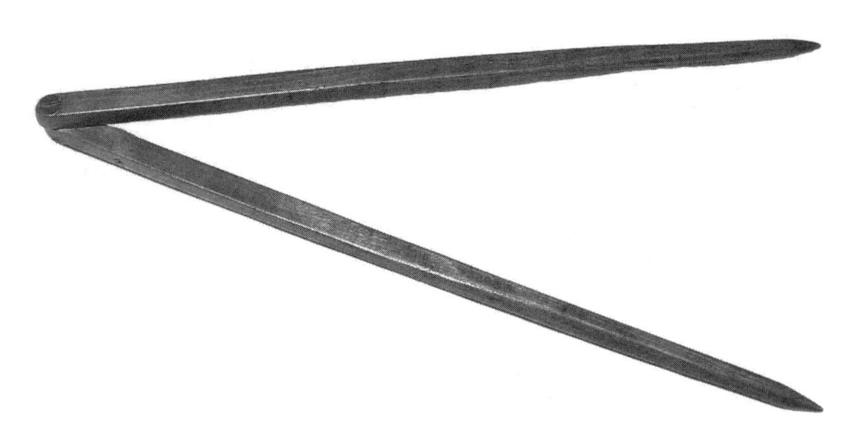

**Fig. 1. A cooper's diagonals for a 14 gallon barrel with an 18" leg.**

is really a gauge) is placed in the already formed barrel that has its bottom in place. See Fig. 2. One tip is placed at the junction of the stave and the bottom, the pivot joint is rested against the belly, and the remaining tip indicates the level where the groove for the lid should be cut.

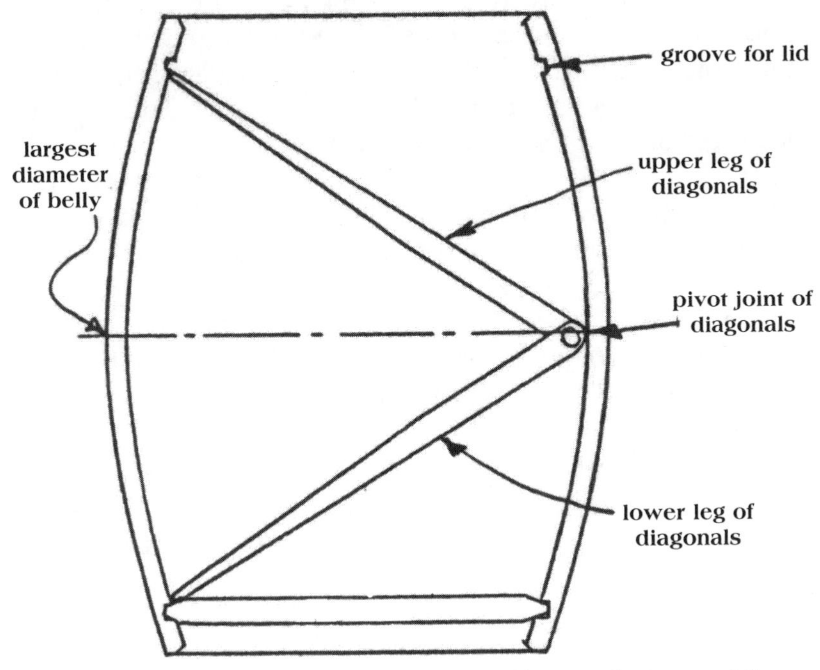


**Fig. 2. Cross-section of barrel showing diagonals in position.**

Using the diagonals as a guide, an experienced cooper can adjust the position of the top croze groove in order to yield the capacity required (within allowable limits). And it can be proven with some calculus, geometry and computer work. The downside is that it is necessary to have a diagonal for each size barrel. Although I'm only guessing, I'd say that the Master Cooper made his set of diagonals using finished barrels that were already checked for capacity. Kind of a backward approach, but nevertheless a perfectly accurate way to do things. Trial-and-error is the antithesis of a calculated design, and although sometimes more time consuming, it is usually deadly accurate.

You will rarely see these diagonals for sale, most likely because of the ease of misinterpreting the wooden ones as worthless. (The English did have a few that were all metal). Such aids as templates and diagonals were probably used only by apprentices, and discarded when experience proved them unnecessary.

With a little study, it can easily be seen why this simple gauge works. If the barrel is bellied-out too much, the pivot joint of the gauge will touch lower in the barrel, and therefore the tip of the upper leg of the gauge will also touch lower. This gives a lower height to the "containing" portion of the barrel (the space between the bottom and the lid), and offsets the increase in diameter created by the oversized belly. If the belly was too "flat" (tending toward cylindrical) the opposite correction would occur. Overly simplistic? To prove it, spend a few days on the calculations or call a math professor at Stevens or MIT. (Jack Whelan, who holds a Doctorate in Chemistry, did the math for me.)

I have mixed emotions about disclosing this rather simple trick for an otherwise mind-boggling operation. I feel information about tools should be disseminated if we are to have them elevated to their proper level. But if I keep doing this, I won't have any jaw-dropping stories left when I give my barrel-making demonstrations. On second thought, coopering has so many colorful and interesting vignettes of man's ability to conquer complexity with minimal equipment, that I don't think I will ever run out of these stories.

# 30

## A CHRISTMAS STORY
## (1987)

An antique tool, like perfume, is a hard gift to pick out for someone. It is a lot more personal than you think. Although you believe you know the person, it is *your* likes and dislikes creeping into the selection that gets you into trouble. However, there is one surefire way of getting it right, and that is to get the intended donee involved, so you can check his reactions. It's not the easiest thing to do, and many times you end up spilling the beans.

I'd like to tell you of one of the best ruses I have ever seen relative to this technique. And I'm happy to say that even though I was the one thoroughly duped, I am now the recipient of the most prized tool in my collection. Prized not just because of its beauty and rarity, but because of the sentiment attached to the way I got it.

It started with a phone call from my son just after Thanksgiving. "Dad," he asked, "have you ever seen a plane like a Stanley 43 that has an iron handle and a lot of fancy filigree all over it?" Well, this was a few years back — B.I.P.M. (Before Iron Plane Mania) — and I really wasn't sure what he was talking about. So I waited with great interest until he got home for Christmas.

When he arrived, he didn't waste any time showing me the plane and asking my help to identify and price it. With

Roger Smith's book just published, it was easy to pick the plane out as the rarest of the Miller patents — the one produced for only a few months in late 1872. Quite a find, for according to Moody's book there were only two or three known to exist. It was a great moment. If I could get this plane, I would finally have *one* piece in my collection that Merc Beitler didn't have.

I found out the retail value from the Iron Plane mavens, who also verified that less than 10 were estimated to exist. Wow! But the appraised price was astronomical. It killed me to think about paying that much for anything, so I rationalized a little. Wasn't a discount warranted here, and wouldn't the money stay in the family anyway? Of course. So I made what I still thought was an outrageously high offer. In my mind it really wasn't an offer, as I could not see how he would even consider turning it down. It was more of a swashbuckling, benevolent gesture — in keeping with the true spirit of Christmas.

*Stunned* was an understatement of my reaction when he hemmed and hawed around. I couldn't believe it. Shock turned into frustration and then to irritation. I quickly ran for the Great Arbitrator. She certainly would straighten this out one-two-three. But no! She thought it best to get more information on something this rare. If I wasn't so aggravated, I would have seen through the whole thing right then, as Doris doesn't know rare from schmare when it comes to tools.

However, knowing how tough it is for my son to sell a great piece, I just wrote it off as temporary insanity. I was sure that in a day or so, with the right song and dance, he would come to his senses and sell it. Wrong again! Finally, I actually gave up and planned my vendetta to get even. Just wait till he asks me to restore the next tool — just wait.

Christmas morning came and I can honestly say there wasn't a trace of vengeance left in my heart. I had completely put the plane out of my mind. And then I was handed a brown paper bag, and everyone stopped doing whatever they were doing to watch me open it. It was the plane.

There are few events in your life that you take to the grave. They never lose their impact, be it joy or sorrow. Being given that plane, with a proud grin from my son, was just such an event. It is my number one piece, and no doubt always will be.

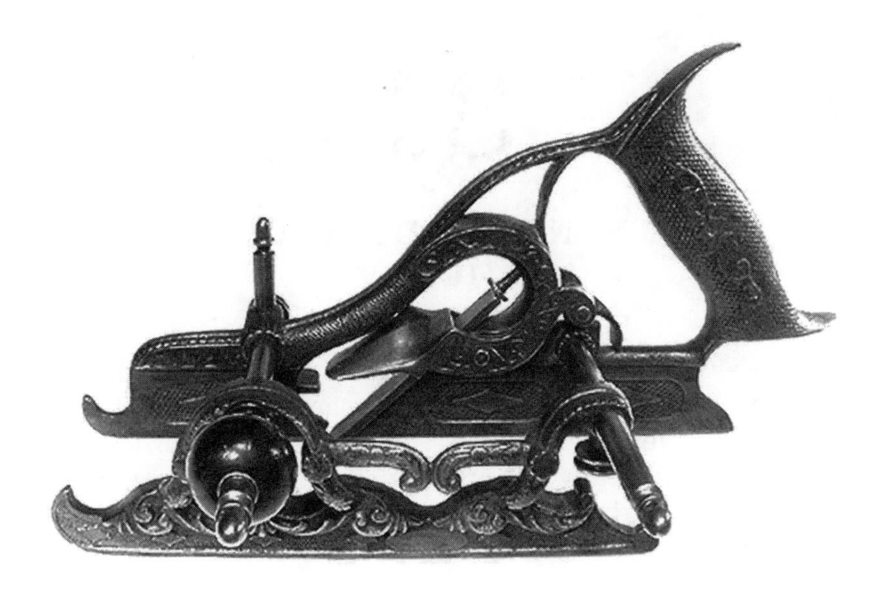

P.S. It hurts me to report this, but Merc owns not one but two such planes.

# 31

## STRANGE BEDFELLOWS
## (1996)

It's only on rare occasions that we, as tool collectors, get interested in business transactions that took place between tool manufacturers. Then we find that they were pretty much like any other businessmen. It boils down to what we see today amongst our lawyers: adversaries in court, and drinking buddies after the verdict. I guess it was that way with some of the more competitive tool makers; the most vociferous being the Stanley and Sargent companies.

I never gave this much thought, until just recently. I was called on the phone to buy a "funny molding plane." I like *funny molding planes*; they generally turn out to be neither funny nor molding planes. What they usually turn out to be is different, and many times rare. Such was the case here, but it took a while to believe it.

The plane was described to me over the phone as "a metal plane with a wood handle, some other metal pieces that fit onto two long rods, and a bunch of cutters in a box." Sounded like a Stanley #45 or possibly even a #55. Now a #55 spurs my interest, as it is more valuable and generally fairly clean (because of a lack of use). As the description went on, I resigned myself to the fact that it was probably a #45. I slowly drifted away from my original interest.

He told me about the screwdriver and the little pamphlet, and the extra set of rods.

"Uh-huh, uh-huh," was my repeated response until the bomb fell. I didn't recognize it as a bomb because at that point it didn't explode.

"The box says Sargent on it," was his rather casual comment. Another, "uh-huh."

Sargent #1080 and Stanley #45 are fairly similar. You might get an argument on this from an avid Sargent collector, or a shrug from a Stanley collector, but a dealer looks at it from the standpoint of how easy it will be to resell. My interest faded even further, but politeness demanded that I allow the gentleman to finish.

He continued with, "It has this almost brand new, round knob up front to help you push the plane." It was worse than what I had thought; it was probably a cannibalized #1080 with a #45 fence, as the #1080 has no front knob. I explained this to the owner only to have him tell me, "But it has the name Sargent on the parts themselves." Now I was somewhat at a loss for words (a quite unusual happening for me). My only retreat was to have him bring it over for me to look at. Maybe I could offer enough for "parts" to keep from hurting his feelings.

A few days later we met. My first reaction was almost the classic, "I told you so." It *was* a Stanley fence all right, but *everything* about the plane was Stanley, even the blades. Well, OK so it's a Stanley #45 in a Sargent box. Not unheard of. But then how do I explain the Sargent markings on the plane and on the paper label on the cutter box? And what about the fact that there is no indication of a Stanley mark anywhere? The biggest puzzlement of all was the picture of a Stanley #45 under the Sargent banner on both the instruction pamphlet and the side of the box! (See picture on the next page.) I thought that Stanley made planes for Montgomery Ward, Sears, and the like, but making planes for their arch enemy! I couldn't believe it. But I bought the plane anyway; it was all there, in good condition, and could be sold to a user.

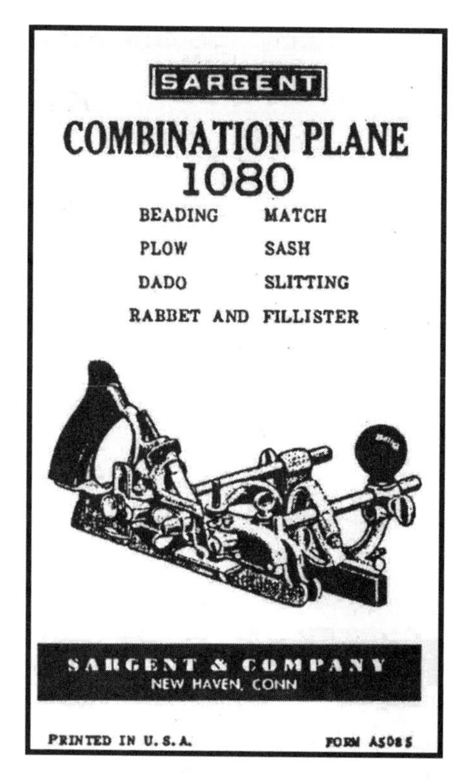


However, my curiosity got the better of me and I decided to find out about this seeming anomaly. The previous owner had called the Sargent company about the plane but wasn't told anything that would explain it. I called the foremost authorities that I knew: the Jacob brothers for Stanley and Paul Weidenschilling for Sargent. There was no question in any of their minds as to what I had.

In 1948, Sargent gave up on the #1080 and ceased production of it. As fate would have it, just after the line was torn down they received a rather large order for #1080s. Rather than reopening and retooling their line, they opted to try to get Stanley to make the planes for them. It was obvious that Stanley couldn't do it economically unless they used their own castings and parts. So the #1080 transformed into the #45, with not too many people any the wiser — or really caring one way or the other.

There aren't many of these hybrids around. The speculation is that Stanley produced only one run for Sargent, and the planes disappeared from the factory floor about a year or so later.

I'm intrigued by the whole episode, and will probably keep this "genetic cross" just to show the peculiarities of the human nature that produced it. I suppose it's just a takeoff on the old adage: "Politics (or business) makes strange bedfellows."

# 32

## YOU WIN SOME AND YOU LOSE SOME (1996)

This story goes way back in my tool collecting days. Doris and I were at Lake George, which was one of our favorite spots then. There was only one activity I treasured more than tool hunting — fishing. At that time Lake George had the peace and quiet that Doris liked and the Northern Pike that made my blood pressure rise.

We never stayed in any place longer than a week, mostly because of my restlessness, and we were scheduled to leave the next day, Saturday. However, there was a giant Flea Market that Sunday. I was told that there would be tools galore at this market; and in those days "tools galore" meant more than rusty wrenches and broken-handled hammers. The thought passed through my mind that it would be a good idea to stay over and "start fresh" on Monday.

I tried it out on Doris. No soap. We had reservations at The Balsams, and she had been waiting for years to go to this one-time world-class hotel near the Canadian border in a setting called the Switzerland of America. I didn't think any degree of arguing would help, so I just mumbled off to my canoe to get in one last fishing adventure.

I felt something big was going to happen on this last outing, but I had no idea how "big" it was going to be. Now don't put this down with grumblings about "another darn fish story." The fish only play a minor role in this drama.

As this was my last try on the lake, I started out close to the cabin and fished for bass. I hit one after my second cast and he felt heavy. Yes sir, this was going to be a good ending to our stay at Lake George. It went all bad from there. The bass dived under the canoe and I reached too far over to keep from snapping the pole. Kerflop, the canoe tipped and everything went into the water. I spent the next few minutes trying to salvage the stuff sinking in the water, along with cutting the line so the fish wouldn't make off with my new pole. It was hectic, and it didn't go unnoticed.

One of the marine police boats that was scanning the lake for infractions, found me in their binoculars. They zoomed over to the rescue. I was cursing the fish, the lake, and anything that was nearby. It must have offended their psyche or something, because the first thing they asked me after they got me to shore was, "May we see your fishing license, sir?" Guess what? I had gotten a five day license and I was in the sixth day. Oh Boy!

Slick talking could not get me out of it; I was going to have to pay the fine. One of the officers explained that if I came down to the magistrate's office I could pay it there, but only if I hurried, as he was leaving for the weekend. An idea started to percolate. Very politely I asked if I could contest the charge.

"Of course," was the immediate reply, "but you'll never be able to hold the magistrate long enough this afternoon; it'll have to be Monday morning." Oh, how bright everything looked at that point.

I sheepishly asked, "Do I get a summons or something?"

"You bet your buppie you do."

Exactly what I needed to prove to Doris that we must stay until Monday or feel the wrath of the long arm of the Law. I had actually pulled it off! Needless to say, I had to move our reservations forward a few days before explaining the sordid details to Doris. Yes, she was irritated, but only until I told her that I had upgraded our room (nothing else was available for the new period). The nagging thought in my mind at that point was: this flea market better be worth it.

Sunday it rained like the Hammers of Hell, and the market was canceled. Come Monday morning, we all sat around waiting for the magistrate. Oddly enough the officers were interested in old tools, and we got into a very spirited conversation about how they were part of our American heritage. I felt with this type of rapport I would surely get off. The magistrate must have had a tough weekend, because when he finally stormed in he didn't want to participate in any tool stories. A couple of fast questions and the verdict: fine and court costs. I didn't feel too bad about the fine, but I almost flipped when I found out what it took to run a "one room schoolhouse" type courtroom. You could have run the Capital Building in Albany for that amount.

You win some, and you lose some. This episode was classified as a solid loser.

# 33

## TOOLS OF THE AMERICAN INDIAN (1994)

This article was written based mostly upon the Lenape people of New Jersey, eastern Pennsylvania, northern Delaware, and southeastern New York. After 1664 they became known as the Delawares. Many thanks must be given to those below for their gracious help in researching original data and correcting my mistakes:

John Kraft, (originator and curator of the Lenape village at Waterloo, N.J.),

Herbert Kraft (author of *The Lenape* — the book from which many of the sketches and other pieces of information for this article were gleaned), and

James Lone Bear Revey, (Chairman of the New Jersey Indian Office).

To keep this article to a minimum, it was necessary to eliminate any discussions of implements that were not tools. The definitions used were: an implement is used to help do something, while a tool is used to help make something.

The thing you might find surprising is the age of these tools. If you look at some of the tools in the Early Archaic Period (8000 B.C. to 6000 B.C.), you find it difficult to tell them apart from those of the early 17th century. See Fig. 1.

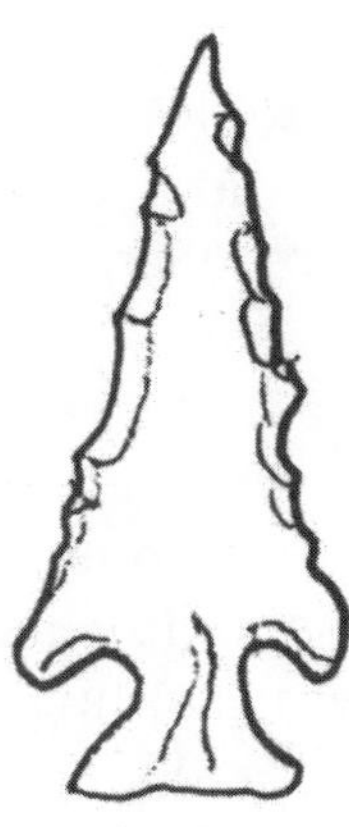

**Fig 1. A spearpoint from the early Archaic Period (8000 B.C.-6000 B.C.). Many tools were made from worn out implements of this shape.**

The materials that were used for tools are about what you would expect: stone, wood, gut, rawhide, sinew, bone, antler, teeth, shell and — one that you might wonder about — copper. Unlike iron, copper could be fashioned in its original condition without smelting. A copper needle, 13" long was found in northern New Jersey, dating around the time of Christ. Of course things changed when the European influence was felt. Iron then became the preferred material.

The only categories of tools that are significant during the pre-European period are: boring tools, edge tools, scrapers, and hammers. Most of the examples of these categories are included. Needless to say there were infinite variations of every tool, as each craftsman had his own style, (not too different from today).

Boring was done by the Indians in a variety of ways. One was very much like how they started their fires — with a **bow drill**. See Fig. 2. They used **pump drills** also, but their most rudimentary hole drilling was done by using a tool, usually made from an old spear point, and turning it by hand. See Fig. 3.

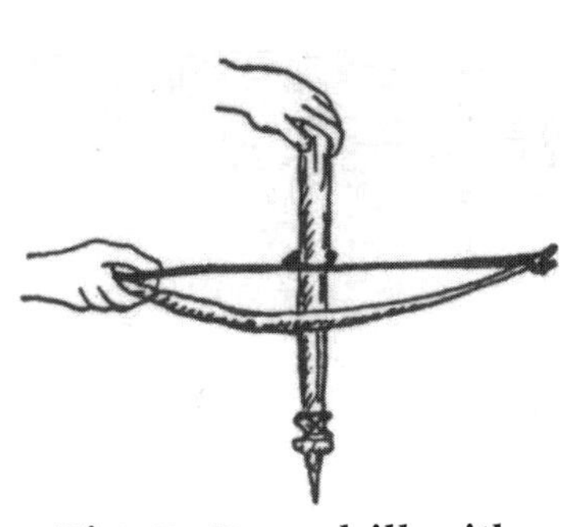

**Fig. 2. Bow drill with reworked spearpoint used as a bit.**

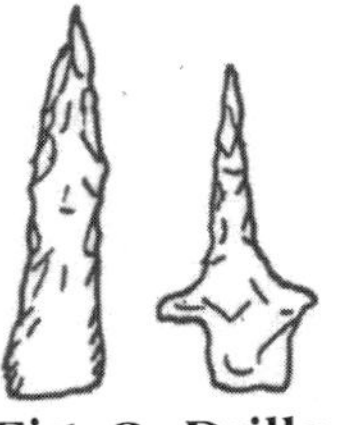

**Fig. 3. Drills made from spearpoints, generally used with handles.**

But what seems almost unbelievable is what they used for drilling in stone: a hollow reed with sand as an abrasive! And if the bow wasn't available, they twirled the reed between their palms. See Fig. 4. Although perforating might not be considered under

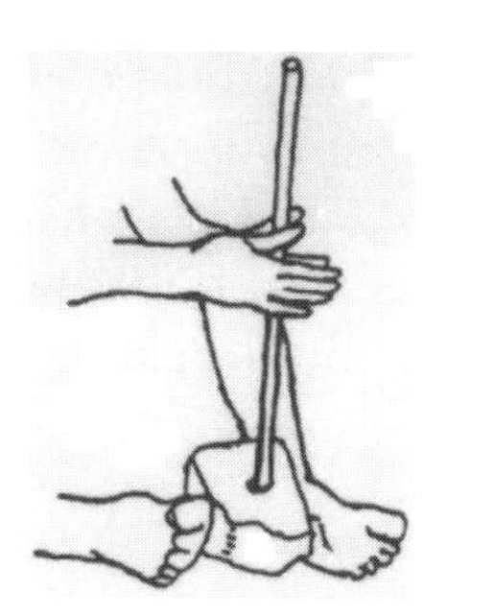

**Fig. 4. Using a hollow reed and sand as a drill.**

boring, it is mentioned here for simplicity. When making holes for stitching and decorating they would use an **awl** made from a bone or an antler. See Fig. 5.

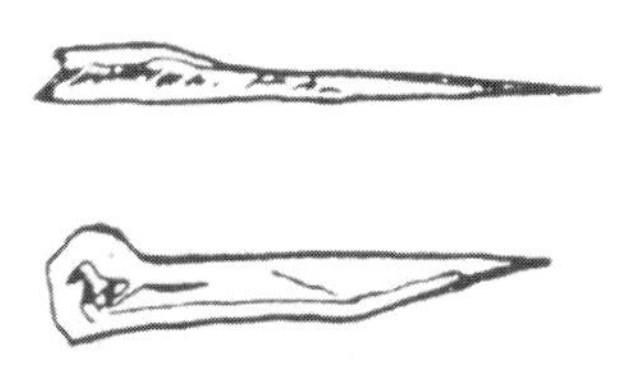

**Fig. 5. Awls made from bone and antler.**

Most of the things that were made by the Indians were done by using edge tools, The **axe** was one of their most important tools. It was used to convert the standing saplings into workable poles for their lodges, travoises, bows, etc. Looking at the axe heads found from thousands of years ago you might ask why they are rarely sharp (as we think of sharp). Although these stones did wear, the consensus is that few were very sharp to start with. The cutting operation was, in many cases, more of a pulverizing technique, although some of the harder stones were brought to an edge sharp enough to cut.

Some of the stone heads had grooves cut in them to help seat the wooden handle, which was bound with a thong. See Fig. 6. These grooves were cut either completely around the head or only 3/4 or 1/2 way around; heads with no grooves were called celts.

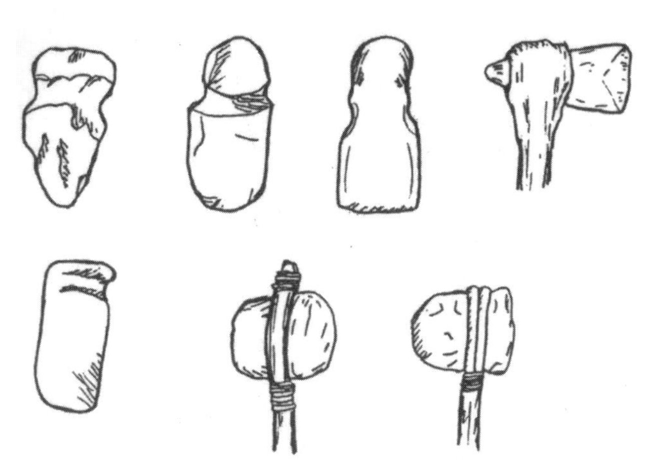

**Fig. 6. A variety of axe heads.**

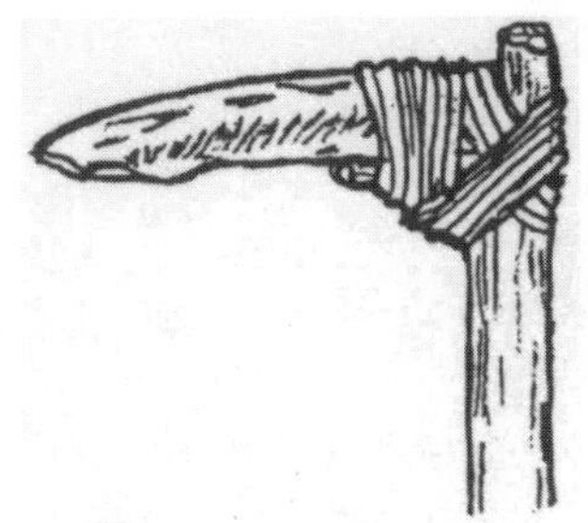
Fig. 7. Stone adze head, rawhided to wooden haft.

With the advent of the iron trade axe, cutting wood became much easier. The longer heads, up to 9", were used mostly by the women for getting firewood. Trade axes were only occasionally used as weapons; the tomahawk was the axe of war.

The adze was very much like the hand adze that later came from Spain and Portugal, except that it was bound with rawhide rather than wedged. See Fig. 7. Early adzes were flat on the bottom side of the cutting edge, and later were improved to be gouge-shaped. Large hollowing-out projects, such as dugout canoes, were not done solely with the adze. Fires were used to make the wood easier to scoop out. Fires were also used in place of the saw, and were utilized to not only fell large trees, but also to buck them into logs for rafts, etc.

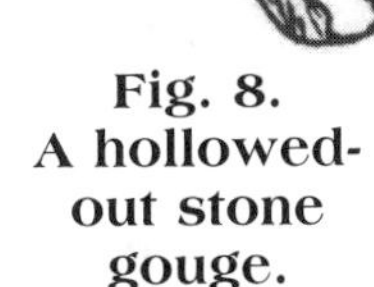
Fig. 8. A hollowed-out stone gouge.

**Gouges** were simply grooved stones, and looked somewhat like our steel gouges, without handles; see Figure 8. Small gouges were probably used to make spoons, while larger ones were used to make bowls.

**Gravers** were chipped stones used for carving and decorating. They differed from small knives as they had no long continuous cutting edge, just a cutting tip similar to our engraving tools. Many of the Indian's implements were highly decorated. As such, the gravers were important tools and were used with great pride. See Fig. 9.

Fig. 9. Gravers chipped from stones.

It is probable that the **knife** was the most important tool of the Indian culture. Originally the knives were nothing more than chipped stones, with elongated edges. They picked stones which would flake easily when chipped, and also hold an edge. Flint was a good example. See Fig. 10. After the arrival of the Europeans, iron and steel knives took over, and were among the first objects traded. The knife that is attributed mostly to the tribes of New England and Canada was the so-called crooked knife (pronounced with two syllables — crook'-ed). See Fig. 11. These knives were generally made from worn out tools such as files and straight razors, and were used mostly for handlemaking and basketmaking. The crooked knife (pronounced with one syllable), with a blade curved at the tip — functioning like our scorp — was used for bowls and spoons. See Fig. 12.

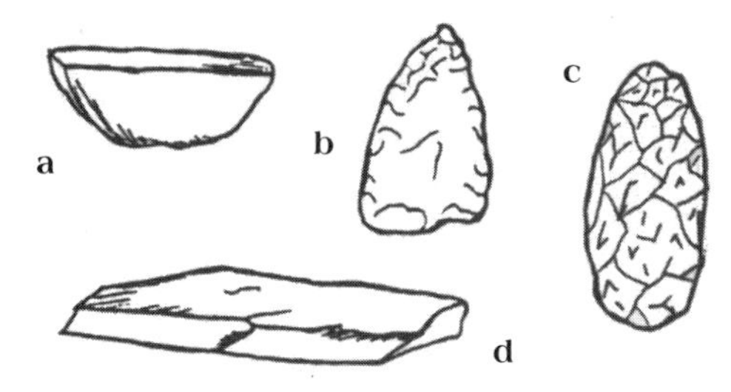


**Fig. 10. Knives: a) halfmoon slate; b) from old spearpoint; c) chipped from flint; d) fractured slab. Types b & c usually mounted in wooden handles.**

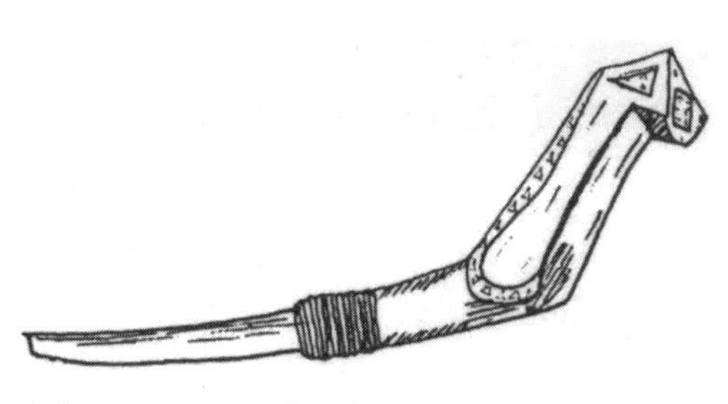

**Fig. 11. Crooked (crook'-ed) knife from an old straight razor.**

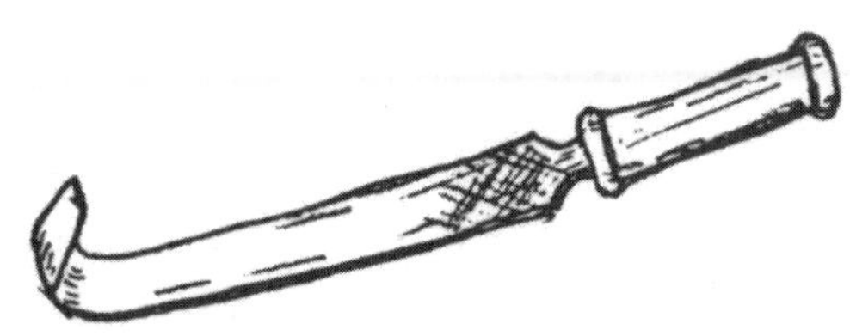

**Fig. 12. Crooked knife from an old file.**

**Scrapers**, even though simple in construction, were necessary to the Indian. Arrow shafts had to be made true for obvious reasons, and the scraping of hides was absolutely essential. See Fig. 13. A small but well used scraper was the sinew

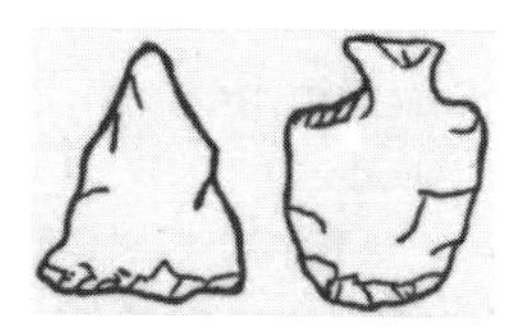

**Fig. 13. Scrapers from old arrow and spear points.**

Fig. 14. Sinew dressers.

dresser, used exclusively for taking the fat off of the raw sinew (ligament). See Fig. 14. An effective scraping tool used for the inside of bowls (after burning) was the split beaver tooth mounted on a wooden or antler handle. See Fig. 15.

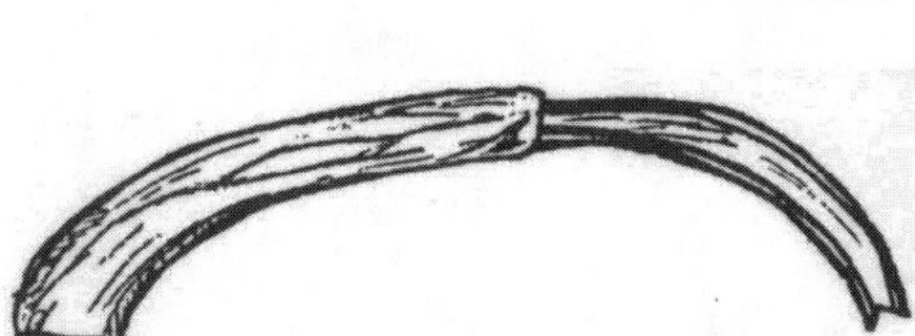

Fig. 15. Split beaver tooth scraper with antler handle.

**Hammers** probably go back in time further than any other tool; the first one being a simple rock. Later they were refined so that they could be used for chipping and pecking other tools. See Fig. 16. Many of the pounding operations, i.e., driving stakes, might have been done with the back side of the axe, as not many hammerheads (that were used with handles) were found. It is also possible that the pounding operations were done with wooden clubs similar to our froe clubs.

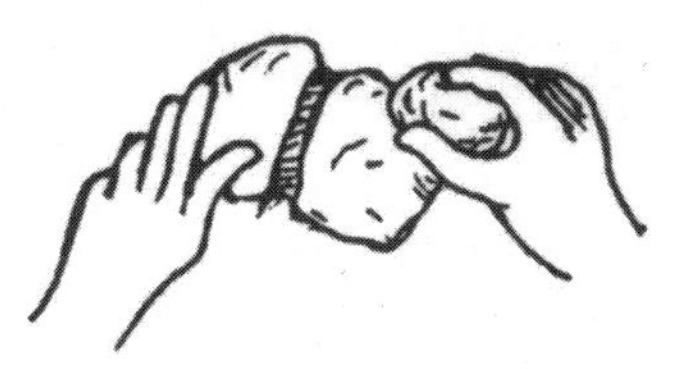

Fig. 16. Pecking an axe head with a hammerstone.

Tools used by the American Indian were rudimentary but effective. One has only to look at some of their artifacts to see what true craftsmen they really were.

# 34

## CANADA, O CANADA!
## (1989)

I love to reminisce. And when someone triggers my memory that brings back a nostalgic event, I couldn't be happier. Just such a trigger occurred at one of our CRAFTS meetings recently, when someone asked me about tools in Canada.

The time was the summer of 1975. Doris and I had reservations in a brand new hotel in Quebec, and we were on our way. As both of us liked back roads, we decided to wander up through the White Mountains and cross the border at an obscure station at Chartierville, in Quebec province. Luck was with us on the way up, and we were able to fill the station wagon with tools and primitives. They weren't hard to find in those days.

As we crossed into Canada, it was tough to figure out where the custom station was. All we saw was a small hut, like the ones that toy soldiers stand in front of. It obviously didn't have a bathroom, for we spotted the custom official coming out of the woods waving his arms for us to stop.

After the usual questions, he asked us about the stuff in the back. I smiled proudly and asked for a Verified List (to clear us with U.S. Customs on the way home). He couldn't believe that we were not going to sell those things in Canada. I tried to convince him otherwise, but to no avail.

He must have been irritated, because he made us turn around and go back to the U.S. Customs for the List.

That was a real Donnybrook, because most custom stations don't check your exit, only your entry — so the U. S. people were checking us for the first time as we entered from Canada! It took a phone call to the guy in the little hut before anyone believed that we were trying to get into Canada, not out of it. They did explain to us the plight of the Canadian tourist merchant. It seemed that the dealers were depleted of antiques that would sell to the American tourists, (probably due to the Expo), and they were forced to come down into the "States" to buy merchandise. Although the U. S. Customs man mumbled something about "antique runners," he gave us the List. It merely read "Various tools and antiques." When I asked if that meager description would suffice at re-entry, he said he felt sure that we would not be returning with them anyhow.

All this got me to thinking that maybe selling some of the pieces in Canada wasn't such a bad idea after all. So, a few minutes later, when we passed the little Canadian hut again, we stopped and asked the customs man if he knew any place to sell a few things. It was as if we had just given him the keys to the kingdom (or a real bathroom). His eyes lit up and he rushed inside to the phone. The phone conversation was in French, but Doris and I got the drift: "Some fat-cat Americans were coming with antiques." He gave me a hand drawn map and off we went.

The roads in that part of the country were not the best in those days, and the ones we followed on his map were hardly roads at all. Finally, we saw two pickup trucks in a yard full of rusted farm equipment, and 5 or 6 people waving. Doris voted to keep right on going. I gave it half a thought, but figured I could always make a quick getaway if necessary.

The Canadians got across to us that they were serious about buying. Such politeness I had never heard, until the tailgate swung open. Then they were faster and more grabby than piranhas. It couldn't have taken them more than a couple of minutes to empty the entire back of that wagon, and I mean entire, luggage, tire jack, first aid kit — everything!

However, the story has a nice ending. Not only did we get our luggage and first aid kit back, (we never did see the jack again), but we were handsomely paid for everything they took. So handsomely that I was for turning back to New England and getting another load. Guess who vetoed that plan? But we did have a luxurious vacation.

# 35

## A BLANKET AUCTION (1991)

No, it's not an auction of blankets. It's an auction of blankets full of stuff. My son, Steve, first told me about them last year. Things up his way (in Maine) are a little more laid back than they are here; and some types of tools are plentiful there. This might account for the rather casual attitude taken toward these tools in the more rural areas. But, if you get a chance to attend one of these auctions, you might not believe what you are seeing.

Picture a chilly morning with everyone standing outside a barn full of auction lots (in this case tools). At some random hour, when there is enough of a crowd formed, the doors of the barn are opened and the auctioneer mounts his stool. There is no P.A. system, so everyone bunches up close for visibility (and warmth).

The first item that you see is a blanket thrown on the ground directly in front of the auctioneer. Then a stream of runners emerge from the barn carrying tools. Each, in turn, holds up his tool; the auctioneer quickly describes it, and then asks for bids. Whether he gets a bid or not, the tool is placed (or thrown) on the blanket and the next runner repeats the same routine with his tool.

It takes a few minutes to grasp the fact that the bidding is cumulative for all the tools on the blanket. Now this technique is used occasionally in our area when a piece doesn't "open" due to a lack of interest. The auctioneer, rather than withdrawing the piece, will put another lot with it, and bid both lots together. But never will he bid 20 or more lots simultaneously as with the blanket auction! There is little chance of keeping track of what the total blanket value is; it just moves too fast. You have to "gut feel" it. Needless to say, the price is very low when this kind of risk is present.

I asked Steve, "How long do they keep throwing stuff on the blanket?" His answer was, "Until it gets too heavy or it reaches $100, whichever comes first." I was too shocked to bid, but Steve wasn't. He got the first three blankets for $75, $85 and $120 — the third blanket had molding planes. The tools from the three lots completely covered the floor of his van. A blanketful is an awesome "boxlot"!

The better items were individually bid on, but I couldn't get interested in anything until I saw the blanket thrown down again. This time I decided to keep a running count of the total value. The blanket hit maximum weight before the $100 limit. There were at least 10 spuds, 10 axes, 5 adzes and who knows what else. The bid was $80 and my tally showed around $150. It seemed to me we should bid, so I poked Steve, but he just shook me off. "The van won't take the weight," was his only comment. I felt that we should make two trips, but by the time I got out this explanation, the lot was sold.

Steve did then agree to come back for a second pick up, so I was in my glory on the next blanket lot. They were all cooper's tools, but they hit the $100 mark before the weight limit, so the runners did not add any more to the fifteen or so pieces that were already on the blanket. Another fellow and I just bid from there.

Steve and I ended up with two vanloads of rather average lots, and about 20 pieces that were real winners including an ivory and ebony hatsizer that was written up in the *Chronicle*. The last lot was the horse weathervane on top of the barn. It was pretty old, and in decent shape. The auctioneer announced that whoever won the bid would have to climb up and hacksaw it down. Needless to say, the bidding was not energetic. Steve won it and promised to cut it down when he came back the next day.

As the farm we were at was somewhat of a historical item in the county, the local "weekly" reporter came out the next day to take a picture of Steve cutting down the weathervane. He made it into an "end-of-an-era" story.

Now here's the wrapup. A movie company, shooting on location nearby, saw the picture in the paper and got in touch with Steve to rent the weathervane. When they came to his shop to pick it up, they saw all kinds of Americana that they "had to have." (Money didn't seem to be an object for them.) So Steve got to pay for all those tools with the rental money. And in a couple of weeks, he got the weathervane and the rest of the Americana back to sell again.

We should all be so lucky!

**"But I said only if it rained."**

# 36

## INEFFECTIVENESS BREEDS RARITY (1997)

The title almost tells the story. But I'd never let that happen. If I did, you wouldn't need the "ole storyteller."

In life, if a thing doesn't work as expected it usually doesn't get to hang around very long. This is especially true of things that are built to perform some function. Tools are as functional as you can get; so, when a tool doesn't perform right it soon becomes kindling or a boat anchor.

In the latter part of the 1800s, innovations and inventions flourished. Patents were easy to come by, and it was nice to have one. It hardly mattered whether the patent represented something that worked or, if it did work, whether it was effective. Some of these patents were great, others dismal failures. Some didn't make it on their own, but were to lead the way for better patents of the future.

Having set the stage with this last remark, I would like to tell you of a very rare, good-looking tool that I came across at a country-style auction. *Country-style* means that there weren't the usual 50 to 100 knowledgeable collectors to compete with. I went to this auction because the list showed almost all low-level tools. I didn't go to buy; I was looking for an auction house that wanted (and could sell) low level. I was getting more and more opportunities to buy collections of this grade, and fewer and fewer opportunities to sell the stuff.

One of the tools at the auction, surrounded by common molders, was a strange-looking double-bodied dado plane. I had marked my list to bid on a few pieces that had the "look" that was selling to the general public. But this double dado was one that I wanted for my collection.

At that moment my memory of the planes in Roger Smith's books was not up to snuff. I relied on my son's advice, "Dad, if *you* have never seen anything like it, buy it." It was a signed, patented piece that I had never seen before; and, the price was right so I bought it. I guess the rest of the audience was as weak in memory as I was, because most everyone stopped bidding at about half the hammer price. The underbidder had no idea what the piece was either, only that the fellow next to him (who left early) told him it was the best piece in the auction.

I felt a little wiggly about being driven up in the bidding by someone who didn't know any more about the piece than I did. Maybe the guys who dropped out early knew what they were doing! But all this changed when the Long Island contingent of collectors arrived about an hour or so after the auction started. They had been to another sale over in Pennsylvania and stopped off at this auction on their way home. One of the Long Islanders recognized the double dado as the very rare Duval patent (Nov. 1869) produced by the Hartford Plane Co., an unlisted manufacturer.

Roger Smith states in his book *Patented Transitional & Metallic Planes in America (1827-1927)* (pages 124-126) that only one example exists! However, he wrote that over sixteen years ago and the Long Island boys were aware of a few more that had shown up since. With such a small number of extant pieces, the plane took on an enormous stature, and I became a hero rather than the lucky stiff that I actually was.

There are two things about this plane that are puzzling: 1) What is the meaning of the number on the heel? and 2) Why so few survivors?

I talked to Roger about the number. The only example available when he wrote his book had the number 1337 on the heel. It didn't seem likely that this was a production serial number. However, my plane has the number 1118 on the heel, which now gives the impression that it is a production serial number. It's hard to believe that they made over 1000 of these planes, and only a few are still with us. Maybe the first digit is a phony. Without it the remaining three digits would represent a more reasonable number produced.

And now to the more meaningful puzzle: Why so few survivors? To figure this out takes a knowledge of what the plane is supposed to do and how it accomplishes this. According to the patent papers, Duval states that the object of his invention is "to produce in one tool all that is required to form grooves of different widths, or of any particular width, according to the thickness of a shelf, or other purposes for which such grooves may be required." However, when you consider that fully closed it cuts a 5/8" groove and fully open it cuts a 7/8" groove, you have to concede that it has a rather limited range, which may be suitable for shelves and such, but not much else.

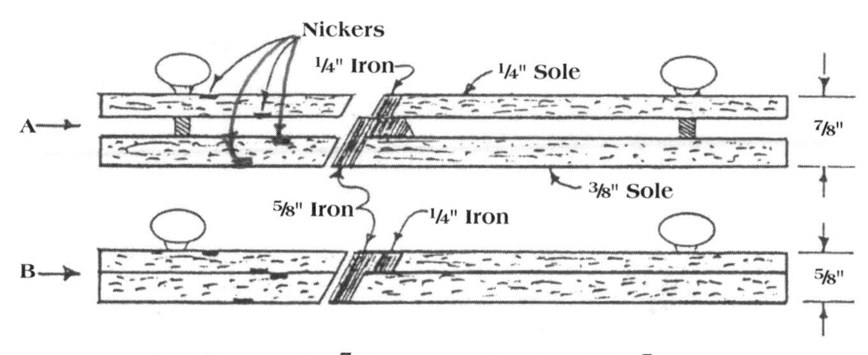


A: Fully open for 7/8" cut; B: Fully closed for 5/8" cut.

**Simplified Bottom Views**

It's questionable why anyone would want to go through all the trouble of setting Duval's two blades to the exact width and depth when standard 5/8", 3/4", and 7/8" dado planes would cover the range, be simpler, and probably be cheaper for all three. If your concern was to match the *exact* shelf thickness, it would be easier to trim the shelf rather than to adjust the dado (particularly in those days when boards were not consistent in thickness anyway).

If you were to take apart the two bodies and use them individually with extra irons, it is possible to get other widths. But most of these widths will not have the nickers corresponding to the iron widths, and cross-grain breakout is inevitable. And, if you use the 3/8" sole, you will not have the advantage of the depth stop (which is on the 1/4" sole). All-in-all, the Duval Patent Adjustable Dado doesn't offer much. It's close, but no cigar.

However, as Roger points out, it may have led the way for Dorn's Patent Combination Dado and finally to Traut's Patent Adjustable Dado. For that we would have to hand accolades to Mr. Duval. However, his plane helps to prove the adage that *ineffectiveness breeds rarity*, and we collectors love him for that.

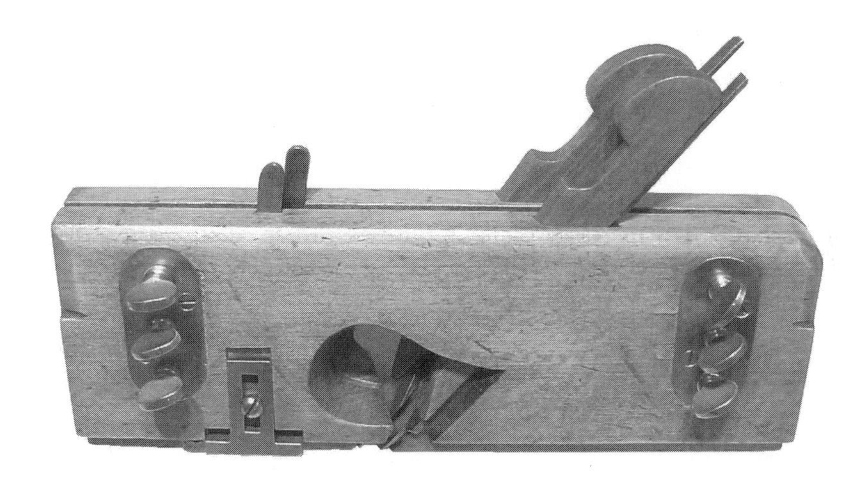

# 37

## THE LONE STAR STATE
## (1990)

Almost all my tales originate in New England, either via personal experience or the cracker barrel environment. But this one happened in the unlikely tool state of Texas.

Years ago, when I was a real person (i.e. before my retirement), I used to make regular trips to Houston to sell for my company. They were always interesting and even exciting, as I managed to hobnob with real Texans and do real Texas things. However, I always lost at the game of one-ups-manship that Texans play in business and in life. To them it was a fun thing; but to me it was frustrating. I rationalized that in business the seller was supposed to lose at golf and poker, but I still wanted to win something besides an order for my company. Well, my chance was soon to come.

On a particularly successful trip, my Texas customers took me to a Prison Rodeo just north of Houston. It was actually held in a prison by the prisoners. It was wild, and I mean wild! We bet on every event, and I lost them all. What was an "eastern city boy" supposed to know about rodeos anyhow?

As the rodeo was a yearly "happening," the merchants in the county took advantage of the enormous crowds and the holiday atmosphere that came with them. They set up booths outside the stadium and sold everything from food to prison crafts. It was just one humongous flea market. We stopped to sample every kind of Texan and Mexican food known to man. While I was picking the jalapeno peppers out of my enchiladas, I spotted a table with some old tools. It was like a letter from home, something I could identify with.

I wandered over with mixed emotions. Should I demonstrate my tool knowledge and let my buddies in on the buy, or should I hog all the tools for myself? They were beauties; all English and in decent shape: spill planes, dove-tailed smoothers and panel planes. We're talking about a time when English tools were in vogue, and reasonably expensive . . . but not these! The vendor apologetically explained that he got them for cleaning out a house. Even so, he must have figured that we were "live ones" and he would try what he felt was a high asking price. After much thought he offered me the entire lot for $150.

Now Texans are not necessarily impressed with "Yankee trading." In fact, just the opposite is what gets their interest. So I took out three fifty dollar bills and handed them quietly to the stunned vendor. That got everyone's attention, particularly since they knew it was not my style. They started questioning me even before we got out of earshot of the vendor. I must say they were quite impressed at the true market value of those old tools. And, as most people are, they were intrigued with the history and functions of the pieces. I was in my glory.

It's not true that Texans buy whatever it is that strikes their fancy, but they do seem to worry less about money, and get more out of life. It didn't take long before they decided to have a tool or two for each of them. They realized that these antiques were personal things to me, and treated them as such when they made their offers to buy them. I reluctantly surrendered my precious cargo at a reasonable profit, and everyone was happy.

So, all those great English tools stayed in Texas, except for one spill plane that I still have. But, more important to me was the thought that brought a smile to my face as I was flying home — I finally won one.

# 38

## ANTIQUE TOOLS, A TRUE COLLECTIBLE (1998)

Chuck Granick recently gave me an article from the *Maine Antique Digest* (March 1982, Eric Greenleaf) that details the life cycle of a collectible. It describes the stages that the collectible goes through from its **junk phase**, through the **collectible phase**, **advanced phase**, **retrenchment phase**, and finally the **mature phase**. It's a real eye opener, even though it discusses collectibles in the generic sense and never once mentions antique tools. It's easy enough to see yourself as a tool collector throughout every one of these phases.

Let's start with the **junk phase**. This is exactly how I got started collecting tools (as I explained in the first article, "The Beginning").

I went to the flea markets and garage sales where tools of this age were looked at as nothing more than junk, or at best "old junk." Even at that they were not plentiful, as most people ended up throwing them out rather than trying to sell them at a pittance.

I had no literature about tools until catalogs from Alex Farnham, Vern Ward, Jack Clouser, and Arnold & Walker came out. Later Bud Steere, the Wings, Bill Neyer and a few others supplemented my growing stack of information.

This phase presented a real grab bag of opportunities. Not too many people knew what they were doing and it made for wonderful, daring, confusing, but exciting times. Tool dealers were almost non-existent at the fleas, with tools coming up in the most unlikely booths. Mistakes were plentiful, but hardly costly. Tool collectors were looked at with a jaundiced eye, as their tastes were suspect. It didn't matter; we were a tough-skinned bunch.

Next came the **collectible phase**. For many different reasons, tool collecting caught on. Both collectors and dealers took notice. Auctions that were composed entirely of antique tools cropped up in New England. Jack Bittner and Lee Murray with Dick Crane were to run the only tool auctions that amounted to anything for some time to come. It was years later that Bud Brown and Al Bates combined to give us the now famous Brown Auction. The two English auctions and the Hurchalla auction were just a twinkle in the eye during these early times.

Jack Bittner was the "grand ole man of tools," complete with dry humor and cracker barrel stories. Dick Crane with bowler hat and bright red suspenders entertained everyone, along with his auctioneering duties. You had a warm feeling coming away from those old-time auctions.

As the word got around about the prices paid for some of the rarer pieces, all kinds of treasures started coming out of the woodwork. This created a significant increase in the number of dealers handling tools. Almost every Americana dealer now carried a dozen or so pieces. They all lamented, "We can't keep these things on the shelf. As soon as they come in, they're whisked away."

It was in this glow that CRAFTS was born. The stories of the original guys are legend. We all wanted to get out from Saturday chores, and a club with a long name was the perfect thing. The tool sales that I held in my shop on Saturdays were becoming zoo-like, and we were looking for a quieter place to gather. We found it in a historic mansion near Rutgers University.

One of the first speakers phoned in that he couldn't make it. I was elected to cover for him.

“What's the subject?” I asked.

“Coopering.”

“I don't know much about coopering, other than the tools that I own.”

“Don't worry, we have a film. All you have to do is show it and your tools.”

I'm sure you can guess what happened. Yep, the film never showed up. And Kooper Kean was born.

CRAFTS got into the auction business in 1979. When they had to pick the guy for auctioneer, they figured they better get someone who talks all the time. There weren't too many choices. I'll never forget my “practice sessions.” They occurred in the car on the way home from work. Sometimes I would get carried away, and would be chanting and ranting right up to the red light. One time, an elderly lady pulled up next to me, looked over at what appeared to be a raving lunatic, and drove her car right through that red light to get away from me.

With the help of Steve Zluky, who kept prodding me on with his cry of “Sell it, sell it!” we did $8580 that first year. Man, were we proud.

Later in this phase the books started to come out. Up to that point all we had was Mercer's rather dry treatise and Eric Sloane's picture book. As Greenleaf put it in his article, “A crucial juncture occurs when someone writes a book. This sets standards and criteria to judge pieces by, in addition to giving the collectible lots of publicity.” Yes, the *Chronicle* was putting out informative articles, but not to the general public as a book does. The books moved tools to a much more respectable position. The shroud of ignorance was lifting and we were delighted with our newfound illumination.

Then came the **advanced phase**. It was now politically correct to collect tools, and everyone tried their hand at it. Speculators came from the least likely places. A year or so later they were asking the dealers to take everything back as they were not “beating the bank.” Clubs cropped up throughout the country from coast to coast. With demand going up, prices followed. We were on the roll that everyone had felt was inevitable.

Somewhere in the grey mist, grumbling started. It came from two diametrically opposed factions. The first group viewed the "Johnny-come-latelies" as unwanted competition. Publicizing and expanding the antique tool market was not to this group's liking. On the other side of the coin were those who in frustration asked, "Why are tools on the bottom of the ladder, compared to other collectibles?" This group actively sought an expanded market.

And, it was not long before tools became a true collectible, complete with international auctions, books detailing the intricacies of each model, and price guides. We had arrived!

The next phase snuck in on little catfeet. We never realized it was there — the **retrenchment phase**. The cry of "Buy only the best" hurt the midrange tools. (The low end was ignored years before.) Condition became the primary criterion, as is the case with all advanced collectibles. Beginners now wanted to start with the high end. Trends that skyrocketed prices in certain categories in the previous phase were reevaluated and brought back down to reality. The really fine tools became quite pricey, and rightly so when you realize how few of them are around. But the so-so tools suffered.

Records show that collectibles that were deserted by their collectors occurred mainly because the supply dried up. Even with the hundreds of thousands of antique tools in the world, the supply will still dry up if we all collect only the best. Only the best is right for some, but certainly not for all, particularly beginners.

But the retrenchment phase doesn't last forever. Almost all other collectibles have gone through it and were made better for it. The **mature phase** is next. Dedicated collectors and skilled dealers take over. As water seeks it own level, so does the level of the collectible during this phase. Some of the problems mentioned above disappear. The low level gravitates to non-tool collectors. The midrange comes back for beginners. The trendy stuff is no longer creating a screw-up in pricing as collectors are now smart enough to know "real" value. Prices climb slowly in a stabilized market. Maybe it's not the same excitement that we had in the early days, but everything changes, and we accept that.

I believe the mature phase is close at hand, if not already here. I only hope that we become mature enough to include collectors of all motivations and styles, and get rid of the dogmatic descriptions of the so-called right and wrong way to collect. Tools appeal to a vast variety of people, and as collectors these people function in different ways. Unless it can be shown that a particular method is causing harm, we should welcome them all.

Yes, we should include those who can afford only the low end, ignore signatures, collect only primitives, collect duplicates, clean up stuff, don't clean anything, collect for function, could care less for function, properly restore missing parts, won't accept any restored parts, pack everything away, and on and on. Tools are too important a link to our heritage to be relegated to a single-track method of collecting.

I'm not sure what the future will bring, but I have a mountain of memories of the past. Tool collecting is, and always will be, a large and enjoyable part of my life. Hope it is for you also.

# 39

## THREE-ARM PLOWS
## (1999)

Who was the first planemaker to come up with a three-arm plow? I am excluding the European three-arms where only two arms go into the body. The concept is not quite the same with these plows. The true three-arm plows such as the Sandusky centerwheel, Ohio centerwheel, Kimberley (English), Brown (Scottish), and Chapin-Rust are all in the latter half of the 19th century and can't be considered as "the first."

Did Israel White, who patented his three-arm plow in 1834, start the whole thing, or did he get the idea from across the river in New Jersey? Could Andruss, who started planemaking in Newark, New Jersey, in 1821, have dreamed up the technique to keep the fence parallel to the skate? Two other Newark planemakers made early three-arm plows. But White's three arm plow was already on the market before I. King first appeared in the Newark 1835 Directory and before Mockridge & Francis started making planes in 1835.

As with any mystery, you have to collect the facts first and then put them together so they make some sense. Unfortunately, in this case it's mostly speculation. Yes, you can come up with a different conclusion, but hopefully, some day someone will come up with some hard evidence. Let's look at the early three-arm plows.

Let's start with Israel White. We know that the patent paperwork shows only the non-bridle style. In addition to that, a broadside advertising the plane came out in November of 1833 showing only the non-bridle style. See Fig. 1. The last few that were produced later by Henry G. White (who took over the shop from Israel White's widow in 1846) were the bridle types. This pretty much says that White's non-bridle came out before his bridle.

**Fig. 1. The non-bridle, three-arm of Israel White. (Courtesy of Leon Kashishian)**

Why the introduction of the bridle to the three-arm concept? My guess is that the center arm of the original non-bridle model (that connected only to the fence and not to the outside arms) allowed too much play under stress conditions. Israel White must have found this out early on, as it appears that he produced his bridle shortly after 1834. See Fig. 2. It's very likely that both styles were produced simultaneously as the serial numbers run from low to high on both styles. Of course he may have serialized each style separately, but as yet there is no evidence of that.

**Fig. 2. The bridle, three-arm of Israel White. (Courtesy of Martyl Pollak)**

Now the tricky part. If we speculate that Andruss came out with his bridle model first, then why would White choose an unproven, possibly ineffective, non-bridle model as his copy? Those who copied designs tried to stay as close as possible to what had already been proven to work. They might modify a detail or two to "skirt the patent" or to claim an improvement, but they would rarely change an entire concept. Also, as you will read below, the details of each plane give the strong impression that the I. King plane preceded the Andruss. But, if King never got started until after the White plane was out, this would also put the Andruss after the White! If you accept the progression from maker to maker that is detailed below, you will have to give first place to White.

So, if Israel White invented the three-arm plow, then who in New Jersey was the first to copy him? For this we have to look at the planes of I. King, Andruss, and Mockridge & Francis. The one that looks to be "elaborate beyond effectiveness" is the I. King. See Fig. 3. The handle is unbelievable, with its two iron castings attaching it to the body (hard to see in the photo). The manner of attaching the bridle to the outside arms also requires a casting that could

**Fig. 3. The I. King three-arm. (Courtesy of Ken Hopfel)**

have been made a lot simpler. The bushing that accepts the threaded center arm is elaborately inset into the body. The method of holding everything rigid, once the fence is positioned, is with an iron strip set into the forward arm and a wing screw through the body to clamp down on it. Not bad theoretically, but expensive.

Now look at the Andruss. See Fig. 4. It lacks the very expensive handle. The bushing sits on top of the body, requiring no inset cutting. A rather nice improvement is riveting through the arms, bridle, and fence all in one shot,

**Fig. 4. The Andruss three-arm. (Courtesy of George Duin)**

giving better rigidity and making the bridle casting much simpler. In short it lacks almost all of the excesses of the King design, which somewhat acts as proof of Andruss following King.

And now look at the Mockridge & Francis plows, the untoted first. See Fig. 5. It has the Andruss bridle but uses a bulky brass casting, which looks almost like a prototype. (Maybe it is.) Screws were used rather than rivets to attach the arms to the fence. This indicates a natural change in plows, where rivets almost always preceded screws. Mockridge & Francis removed the front arm iron strip and substituted a lock wedge, which was less expensive. The plane has a nut on the center arm. This centralizes the locking pressure and puts a portion of it onto the rear arm. It might have come as an afterthought when the single forward wedge wasn't doing the job, particularly when the rear arm started to wear. It can be seen that the simplification continued as Mockridge & Francis took costs out of the Andruss design.

**Fig. 5. The untoted Mockridge & Francis three-arm. (Courtesy of Martyl Pollak)**

Finally the Mockridge & Francis toted plow. See Fig. 6. The screws attaching the arms to the fence are no longer screwed through the bridle, as in the untoted model. The arms are now screwed to the fence in the same way as any normal plow. The much simpler steel bridle just sits in the mortises in the arms (a cheaper design). There is no wedge or front arm thumbscrew lock. The fence arms are now mortised into the fence, which helps to keep them square to the fence. The need for mortising indicates that there must have been a problem in keeping the arms square to the fence, the very thing that this bridle concept was supposed to lick. As with the untoted model there is a nut on the center arm, which is the only way to lock the fence setting. As this nut was replaced on this particular plane, it could be questioned whether it was there originally and then lost, or was never there to start with. It's not reasonable for a plow plane to be designed with "state-of-the-art" detail and not have a way to lock the arms. So I think it's safe to consider the locking nut design as original or an early afterthought. It would appear that in some areas the simplification went a little too far in this final design. That was probably its death knell.

**Fig. 6. The toted Mockridge & Francis three-arm. (Courtesy of Rick Anger)**

There it is: the White three-arm, non-bridle plow, then the White bridle, then the King, then the Andruss, then the

Mockridge & Francis untoted, and finally the Mockridge & Francis toted. It's interesting to note that almost every change down through time, and from one maker to another seemed to reflect a need to simplify a costly design. There were some changes that addressed a possible ineffectiveness, but they were not as plentiful as those concerning cost.

I. King was only in business for two years after 1835 and Andruss only survived 5 or 6 years after his three-arm came out. Today very few of these planes are extant: one by I. King, 2 or 3 by Andruss, less than a dozen by Mockridge & Francis, and a dozen or so by White. The bottom line for these early three-arm plows is that they didn't seem to be worth the extra cost, as their advantage was slight, if at all. Most ineffective products usually end up being the rarest pieces in any collection. The early three-arm plows fit that bill perfectly.

# 40

## WHAT WE DO FOR TOOLS
## (1997)

Collectors will brave almost any kind of weather and endure almost any kind of hardship to pursue their treasures. Talk about your mail carriers with appointed rounds, collectors have it all over them. There is only one problem with this somewhat masochistic conduct: some of us are married and expose our spouses to this nutty behavior. Such was the case a few years back when Doris agreed to go on a "tooling hunt" with me.

She was aware that these forages usually took three or four days, but we always had a nice time (when she wasn't waiting for me to consummate a tool deal). So off we went up the Delaware River, bouncing from one shop to another and stopping at all the pickers that I had lined up.

I don't remember how I was doing huntingwise as the whole affair is blurred over with the events that followed. That night was burned into Doris' memory. Even to this day I still hear about it.

The first evening out we stopped at a wonderful restaurant for dinner. There was a motel attached to it overlooking the Delaware. It was a great spot, and I anticipated sitting on the porch of the room and drinking in the spring air. But there was no room! The owners were in the process of selling the place, and had closed the motel temporarily. We asked about another spot, but to no avail. It seemed that it was a special weekend of some kind; I think it was the opening of trout season. I phoned what few motels there were in the area, but no luck.

We weren't that far from home and could have easily made it in a few hours. Cancel a tooling hunt? Never! Sleep in the car? To mention that would have been perilous in the frame of mind that Doris was in. What then?

One of the locals slid up to me as if the info he was about to release was of international importance. There was a hunting and fishing lodge nearby, and he would make a call for me if I wanted. I could hardly say no under the circumstances. Yes, they had a room, but only if I hurried. He gave me directions to get there that bordered on a map for an archaeological dig. My head was spinning and I knew I'd never make it in time considering the warning given by the "desk clerk." The local fellow was a cousin or something to the owner, so I prevailed upon him to get his relative to hold the room for us.

He called to find out that the only way they would do it was if I gave him the money. "No credit card machines?" I asked. Just a dirty look in return. The room was so cheap that I felt it was worth the shot, so I did it. "Now," he told us, "you can come to the big party that's going on this evening in the ballroom."

Our newly found friend took us into the "ballroom" where we were introduced to the crowd. It was some type of geriatric club; Doris and I were high schoolers in comparison. I won't comment on the evening other than the booze was cheap for the admission price.

As early as we could leave without hurting anyone's feelings, we beat it. The few drinks I had worsened the nearly incomprehensible directions to the lodge. It took forever to get there. But finally the huge deer antlers hanging cockeyed from the signpost (lighted by a large, shaded bulb) came into view. Doris was starting to get apprehensive as we approached a quonset hut with the name of the lodge burned into an old board. I went inside.

"Everything is taken in the *main lodge*," he explained, "but we kept one room for you in the *barracks*." I imagined the worst, and that's exactly what I got. The rooms were sectioned with sheetrock that was on one side of the studs only. The light was run in on an extension cord from an outlet in the hall. There was no closet, sink, toilet, or anything — just a window, a door, and a bed that could hardly be counted as a double.

I went out to the car to advise Doris that sleeping in the car would probably suit her better. To my surprise, she stormed into the hovel and made ready for the night.

It was awful! The snores and coughs could be heard from rooms as far as three and four away. The doors kept slamming all night. I couldn't understand how Doris could put up with it. Whenever I mentioned that we ought to just leave, a wry smile came across her face and she merely said, "Why would you want to leave such a wonderful place as this?"

Just when I had gotten used to the snoring, and the doors had stopped slamming, some lunatic came running down the hall, banging on everyone's door, and shouting, "Get up, get up, the Day of Reckoning is here!" This was the last straw. We left.

After an hour the sun came up, and we stopped at a diner for breakfast. Neither of us talked about the experience. Doris had that knowing look. She was sure I would never let that happen again, tools or no tools!

# 41

## THERE IS ALWAYS A TREASURE LURKING (1997)

Recently I went to the Jersey shore on a business trip. Whenever I'm out of town I like to stop at the local antique shops to see if there is a treasure lurking somewhere. In the past few years there have been very few treasures, but hope springs eternal.

After striking out in all the shops, I was finally given a lead by one of the proprietors. I don't have to tell any tool collector how most of these leads work out. When you hear, "They have so many tools, it'll blow your mind," it generally ends up with a couple dozen broken and rusty pieces. And when they mention only one piece that they think they saw, you can almost forget about it. That wasn't the case that day. The one piece, "a thing with big wooden screws," turned out to be a handled plow plane.

Even with all the schmutz on it, I felt the wood was rosewood. I didn't recognize the signature — Sheldon & Osborn Mfg. Co./Birmingham, Ct. — so I considered the plane worth a star or two. Incidentally, some of the plane books spell Osborn with an "e" on the end, but there was no "e" on the plane. There are records of families with both spellings in the area. The historical people believe they are the same, and that the “e” was added later when they had money and decided to “class-up.” At any rate I bought the plane.

When I looked up Shelton & Osborn, which was only in the Third Edition of the Pollaks' book, I found them briefly described as: two plow planes known, one ebony and one cocobolo. The ebony one triggered my memory. I recalled auctioning that plane in 1989 for $2300, and, like mine, it didn't even have ivory tips! I didn't put too much faith in the one described as cocobolo, as many woods that have a rosewood look about them are misidentified as cocobolo. Some dealers in the US and the UK still say the lignum vitae heads of Sheffield braces are cocobolo. Even Stanley occasionally used Brazilian rosewood, instead of the catalog-listed cocobolo, for tool handles and drill handles. But I'm drifting.

The wood in the body of my newly acquired plow plane looked like rosewood, but when I cleaned it up it became a brilliant cherry color with darker striations. It was truly beautiful! I guessed it to be Honduras rosewood as it was much too light in color for Indian or Brazilian. But when I stripped all the metal off the body I could tell it was not Honduras rosewood. It was far too light in weight, which also threw out any possibility of cocobolo.

I looked at the grain under magnification on the nose of the plane, where a good cross section was available. It was the exact same puzzling section that I had previously seen on Sargent's VBM handles. So I dragged Paul Weidenschilling (“Mr. Sargent”) into the quandary. He found out that Sargent called this wood East India mahogany. Well, there is no such tree as East India mahogany; it had to be a nickname. And that it was, as Constantine lists Andaman padauk (peh-dook) as being called East India mahogany by the old cabinetmakers. This was logical, as the source of this species is the Andaman Islands off the east coast of India, and most of its variations look like mahogany.

OK here is where the history buffs can get into this. I searched my Connecticut map for the town of Birmingham, and guess what? There is no Birmingham! The Connecticut Historical Society told me that, “Birmingham was located at the confluence of the Naugatuck and Housatonic rivers." It didn't take long to figure out that Birmingham is now called Derby. The Derby Historical Society confirmed this and filled me in on George W. Shelton & Lyman Osborn.

Both families were well respected in the area. The town just across the river from Derby is still called Shelton, and a recreational forest adjacent to Derby is now called Osborndale. The two men started their business in 1854 in the manufacturing borough known as Birmingham, which was a part of the town of Derby. (Birmingham was completely absorbed by Derby in 1889.) The workshops in the village were predominately financed by New York City entrepreneurs. Shelton and Osborn started making parts and novelties from "wood, ivory, brass, gold, silver, copper, tin, and other metals," but by 1858 were making only metal hoops for skirts, which became a big product in the area. No record exists of them ever making planes.

All this history was fine, but the identification of the wood was still bothering me. So I asked the Forest Products Lab in Madison, Wisconsin, to do a micro-section. They confirmed it to be padauk.

At this point I was totally hooked on this maker. What was he doing making planes out of padauk? My search took me to Bob Baker in Mattawan, Michigan, probably the foremost antique tool maker and restorer in the world. He has restored eight Shelton & Osborn plow planes. I also checked out five similar planes, including one owned by Arnold Peterson, a Historical Society member in the Derby area. Here's what I found out.

The Shelton & Osborn mark is known to appear only on very fancy plow planes. And there aren't many of those. One owned by Ron Pearson has ivory tips and ivory nuts. The woods of these planes are all premier: Ceylon ebony, Macassar ebony, Brazilian rosewood, East India rosewood, Turkish boxwood, possibly cocobolo, and now of all things — padauk! I have yet to see another antique plane of any kind made from padauk. All the knowledgable collectors I queried agreed. Although Andaman padauk and African padauk are gorgeous cabinet woods used for the most prestigious trims etc., some variations might have had too much interlocking grain or were too open grained for production planemaking. (I suspect that they didn't use mahogany for the same reason.) However, in the 20th century Sargent and Union did use padauk for a short time, but only for plane handles.

There are two schools of thought as to who made these planes. Bob Baker and a few other collectors feel that they were made by DeForest, who was located right next to Shelton & Osborn (in fact, they used the same mill race). The nut profiles and other characteristics prompt this speculation. It makes sense because DeForest went overboard on premier planes. He claimed to have some of zebrawood, although none have surfaced. He also offered a "handled ivory plow plane with solid gold nuts and washers, 22 carats fine, golden tips on arms and golden mounted, $1000." None have ever been reported as being made. What cabinetmaker could blow $1000 on a tool in the 1850s?

On the other hand, David Carver, the Derby Historical Society's photo archivist who has done research on the Birmingham companies, believes that Shelton & Osborn made their own planes. His records reflect that they were a close competitor of DeForest. You as the reader have a chance to play detective and pick your own culprit. Here are some ideas and clues:

1. Shelton may have had a mailing list of guys with money who bought "executive toys." Remember he started out selling wood and metal novelties. DeForest may have used him as a distributor for the high-end stuff.

2. Shelton had lathes and other woodworking equipment and employed men who had the skills to make intricate parts. It's not unreasonable to believe that he could have made a limited number of planes.

3. Shelton was felt to be competitive enough that he may have copied DeForest's plow planes just for the "hellovit."

4. Shelton's original wood novelties required him to have exotic woods on hand which he may have used for plow planes.

5. DeForest was alleged to have had a licensing problem and had to take his name off some of his planes. Perhaps he sold them to Shelton just to get somebody's name on them.

6. DeForest was always advertising some rare material for his planes, such as zebrawood, gold, etc. Perhaps this was to satisfy a growing one-ups-manship among the premier cabinetmakers.

7. And lastly, there is the possibility, however unlikely, that DeForest copied the designs of his planes from Shelton. I say unlikely because DeForest is listed in the 1850 census as producing 8,000 planes, while Shelton & Osborn weren't even chartered until 1854 and we have no record they produced planes. Both companies were heavily into hoops for skirts and out of other products by 1858.

Maybe someday we will be able to solve the mystery. At any rate, this shows that there is always a treasure (and a good story) lurking somewhere.

Note: Thanks to Rita Breeze, Curator, David Carver, and Arnold Peterson of the Derby Historical Society. Without their research I would still be scratching my head.

# 42

## A ROSE BY ANY OTHER NAME
## (2000)

It was a cold, wintry night in New Britain, Connecticut, many years ago. Around a poker table, next to the fire, sat five influential men of the area: Alix Stanley (Stanley Rule and Level), George Sargent (Sargent & Co.), George Trask (Union Mfg. Co.), Linson DeForest (DeForest Co.), and George Shelton (Shelton & Osborn Mfg. Co.). They all lived reasonably close to one another and this was their semi-monthly poker game, this time at George Shelton's house in Birmingham (now Derby).

"Hey, I have a good story to tell you guys about some wood that we can all use for our planes," mumbled Mr. Shelton. (He was known to all as the "Mumbler.")

"Tell your story some other time; I'm losing," shot back Mr. Stanley.

"Oh, for God's sake Alix, let ole Mumbles tell his story," Mr. Sargent broke in.

"Yeah, I need wood. Rosewood is just getting too blamed expensive," was Mr. DeForest's contribution. Mr. Trask, the "Silent One," said nothing.

"OK, OK, but don't interrupt, I think we can all profit by this deal," said Shelton. "Over in India, or on some island off the coast of India, there's a bunch of trees that are ours for the asking."

"What the deuce are we going to do with trees? I thought you said you knew where there was some wood," interrupted Stanley.

"Give him a chance Alix," was the shocking remark from the Silent One.

Shelton continued. "Well they're trees now, but I know a contractor who will have them down and into lumber inside a couple months if we give him the capital to get started."

"Go on, go on, now it's starting to sound like something." "Wait a minute, what kind of trees are they? We can't use just any wood."

"The natives call them padauk, but we can call them anything we want. They look like a cross between mahogany and rosewood."

"Padauk? That's no darn good as a name. You'll have to come up with something better then that."

"Well, it looks like mahogany, and it comes from the islands off the east coast of India. How's East Indian mahogany?"

"Is there such a tree?" straight-arrow George Sargent asked.

"Naw, but that's what makes it perfect. It will be something new that we can ballyhoo the heck out of."

A reasonable pause and then: "I'm for it." "Me too." "Count me in." "Yeah, OK with me." Another pause, but longer, and then, "Well Trask, are you in or out?" "In."

And so was born the era of East Indian mahogany, Pterocarpus dalbergioides, commonly known as Andaman padauk, from the Andaman Islands off the east coast of India. The planemakers used it for handles and knobs, but padauk was also used by cabinetmakers for decorative purposes, such as the elaborate panels in Pullman Sleeper Cars. (Cabinetmakers also used other species of padauk.)

Shelton even made an entire plane of padauk in his one-ups-manship of DeForest. (See previous chapter.) Union Mfg. Co. used it when other woods were not available. Stanley substituted it occasionally for the smaller rosewood and cocobolo knobs. But Sargent jumped in with both feet and listed it in his catalog as East Indian mahogany. Almost his entire VBM line had this good-looking wood in handles and knobs. However, as the islands became logged over, the supply dwindled. Sometime in the early 1920s, Sargent replaced padauk with a true mahogany.

Note: Please don't write in about the anachronisms or my fictional character descriptions. I wasn't at that poker game (although Chuck Granick claims that I'm old enough to have been there).

**"Me thinks I will call it the shop smith."**

# 43

## SPREAD THE WORD
### (2002)

There have always been three schools of thought about spreading the word on antique tools (or any collectible for that matter). First, there are the folks that want to keep everything close to the vest, as "the less people who know about the collectible, the easier it will be to collect." Then there are the opposites, who feel that "as the number of collectors grows, so will the value of any collections" — the supply will undoubtedly dwindle, and the demand will increase. And of course there is the third group who, for whatever reason, could care less either way.

I have always been of the second school, perhaps too much so, as this story shows. The more knowledge I gained about antique tools, the more interested I was in letting the world know it. I also felt that if I could introduce more people to collecting, or just plain buying antique tools, I would be a more successful dealer. As a result, there wasn't a local hardware store that didn't have a display of some of my tools that did not meet my standards for sale. And any establishment that hung old tools on its walls as decoration was fair game for my salesmanship.

I would happily barter tools for other tools or tools for meals if the establishment was a restaurant. The only Chelor I own is the result of a trade with a restaurant for a mess of stuff that filled their entire wall panel. I wasn't always successful. Sometimes the owners weren't around or weren't interested in changing what they had. I was happy with the successes that brought me an occasional treasure.

Trading tools for meals calls for some finesse. I usually limit myself to restaurants where Doris and I are not known and then work the trade after Doris has left the restaurant. However, sometimes salesmanship gets the better of me.

Some time back, Doris and I were in one of the nicest restaurants on Lake Hopatcong in New Jersey, only miles from our home. We had eaten there before and were somewhat known by the staff. The walls were adorned with primitives, Americana, firearms, and tools — none of which I wanted. But there was a blank spot on the wall where they had just taken down a badly water stained picture. It was a perfect place for some "junkers" that I had in the back of the wagon. Although it broke the rules, I couldn't waste the opportunity and started discussions with the manager right around dessert time.

The look I got across the table from Doris was enough to make me choke on my apple pie. The manager, however, thought it was a terrific idea, as now he would not have to look for anything to cover that bare wall. What to do? Two meals for a box of junkers! How could anyone resist?

When the manager was called away, Doris let me have it: "charity case, embarrassment, overzealous" and on and on. Somehow the waiter overheard part of it and went straight to the manager who recognized that the situation called for tact and rose to the occasion. When he returned to our table he matter-of-factly said, "I think the best way for me to handle this on the books is for you to pay for your meals, and then give me an invoice for the tools — which I will pay you now in cash. And if the two numbers are the same, so be it." What a clear-thinking man. It went down fine with you-know-who.

So to this day, I have tools in three restaurants in New Jersey that were handled in pretty much the same manner. Although I left my card in all three restaurants, as I have in the numerous other places to which I have given or sold tools, my memory says that I have gotten very few leads from any of them. But it doesn't matter because it fits my program of spreading the word about antique tools.

Antique tool collecting is now too big to keep close to the vest. It is well known internationally, and with the increasing number of tool auctions, tool books, and articles in national magazines, the secret is gone forever. So let's all get on the bandwagon and boost the prestige of antique tools. Every local library and Historical Society would love to have a presentation. There are so many of you that have collections that would fill the bill, it shouldn't be hard to ballyhoo our beloved hobby. Try it. You might love it!

**"I think it's some kind of shovel, but the hook on the end puzzles me."**

# 44

## BETTER LATE THAN NEVER
## (1997)

Is it really better to be late than not to show up at all? Here are two cases from the standpoint of the tool collector, each taking an opposite point of view.

**Case 1:**

You have every good intention of getting up at 4:30 a.m. to go to the flea market, but the partying the night before takes away some of your get-up-and-go. In fact there is very little get-up and no go at all — until 8:30 a.m.

However, when you arrive at the flea market you make a beeline straight to where your "secret" dealer always sets up. An appalling number of people surround his booth, and you tell yourself that they couldn't be tool buyers, not this late. You don't recognize any of the crowd and feel that there is still a chance, as this dealer sometimes sets up late and is missed by the swarm of earlybirds.

As you get closer, you can see a rosewood plow plane in the hands of a potential buyer. He is studying it as if his life depends upon this purchase. The tag is hanging from the wedge clearly showing the price to be $100! Good grief, what is he hesitating about? The plane is in superb condition, and the knot in your stomach gets larger when you hear the dealer say, "And there are a bunch of these here cutters that go with it."

"Well, yes but I've seen these planes go for a lot less than this," is the remark from the buyer.

"Yeah, but this one is in mint condition and it's got a name on it," is the dealer's response.

"Will you take $75?"

You're thinking, "Stand your ground, stand your ground, don't take the $75. I'm willing to give you the whole $100." But those words stay choked down. A more aggressive type may have blurted them out in desperation, but you feel this would be impolite and wouldn't want anyone doing that to you.

After what seems an hour of agonizing delay, the dealer finally says, "I got here late today and all the collectors have been through, so I might as well sell it to you for $75. I don't want to go home with it." CRASH, your heart falls to your stomach. If only you hadn't had that second cup of coffee, if you hadn't taken so much time finding a closer parking spot, if, if, if.

You snuggle up to the guy who bought the plane the minute he leaves the booth and is out of earshot. "Do you want to sell that plane? I'll give you a nice profit."

"Naw, I always wanted one of these to put on my desk. This one's kinda nice. I think I'll keep it."

"I'll give you twice what you paid for it!"

"Are you a collector or something? This plane must be worth more than I thought. Thanks anyhow."

After that you wander aimlessly around the market and return home empty-handed. But the incident, and your lousy luck, keeps replaying itself in your mind. Finally you say to yourself, "Why did I even go today? BETTER *NEVER*, THAN LATE."

**Case 2:**

You have decided to invite your wife to go with you to the flea market on Sunday, and then have a nice lunch somewhere. Yes, you won't get started until 10:00 or so, but what the hay, this is going to be a day out with your loved one, not necessarily a tool-hunting day. (Y-e-a-h R-i-g-h-t.)

You enter the market with an attitude of complete abandon. You are carefree and not totally absorbed in finding a tool treasure. (Y-e-a-h R-i-g-h-t.) It's "interesting" wandering around at 11:30. You see people that you never noticed before. You stop to talk to all your favorite dealers, knowing full well that anything good is long gone.

Then your wife finds you at one of the booths. She calls you aside and asks if you saw the plane down at the end of the aisle. "I haven't been down there yet, but it can't be anything good or it would be gone by now," you reply.

"It's in a box and has lots of extra parts. It looks new, but it's old like the ones you have."

"Well maybe I better take a look. Where did you say it was?"

HALLELUJAH, who would have believed it! The dealer got there late also and had just set up. You are the first to see this gem. He is a furniture dealer and had to take this "thing that looks like a woodworking tool" in the last lot that he bought. But he feels it's worth at least $100. "How about $75?"

"Sure, why not?"

Your wife is smiling, because she knows that the profit from this transaction means lobster and champagne for lunch. And you know: BETTER *LATE*, THAN NEVER.

# 45

## JUST WHEN YOU THINK YOU'VE SEEN IT ALL (2001)

About a year ago I received a call from a fellow that told me he had "a slew of levels." We have all had such calls, and we know the percentage of them that turn out to be nothing. But we live in hope, so I went over to look at his "slew."

The slew amounted to six; two without vials, one that a hungry mouse had for lunch, and three other cheapies. He immediately perceived my disdain and grabbed the only one of the bunch that was saleable (a Stanley No.0), and gave me a forlorn sales pitch. "Look at the stuff this one has on its side, that ought to be worth something." Stuff on the side, what the devil was he talking about? But there it was: an anodized pair of aluminum plates, an on-off switch and a nametag. Wow! Could it be one of the illuminating levels?

Nope, no light anywhere, so I looked at the nameplate to get a clue. A nice neat commercial plate that read: Designed

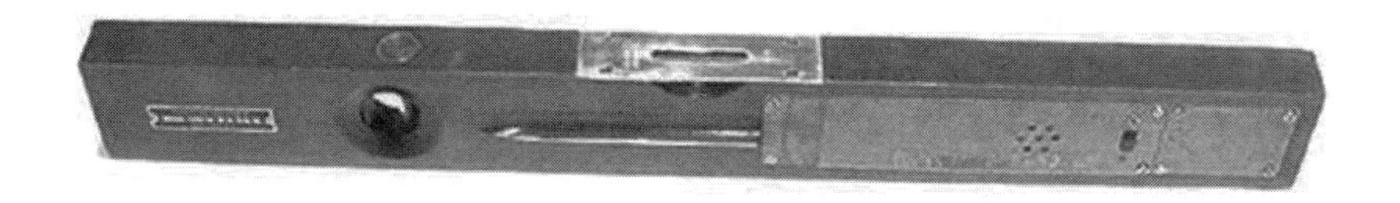

and developed by/AMERICAN FOUNDATION FOR THE BLIND/New York, N.Y.

My first reaction was that this was one of those joke gifts, where someone takes a label from something else and puts it on the gift. However, it seemed that they went to a lot of trouble, as the anodized plates had some Braille scotch taped to it. Could it be real? What would a blind man be doing with a level? . . . And so started a quest that prompted the title of this article.

Once the level was disassembled, it was easy enough to see that: 1) it was truly a level for the blind, and 2) it was modified by Stanley to the specifications of the American Foundation For The Blind. In the factory cutout pockets were a battery, two mercury gravity-vial switches, and a buzzer. The wires were broken, and the solder joints were corroded. But a little cleaning and soldering had the level buzzing away. Only when it was dead level, and both mercury switches were in their inoperative positions, did this baby shut up. At the slightest tilt, one or the other of the mercury switches activated the buzzer.

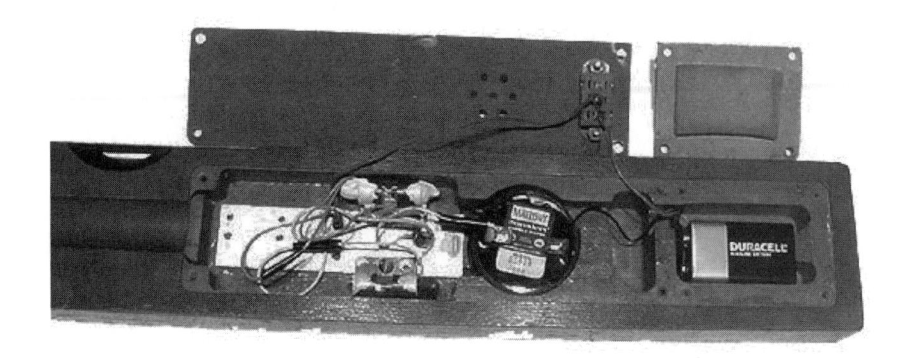


One last thing to do. Figure out what the Braille said. I went to the Internet and found the Braille alphabet and it's sounding combinations. Nothing worked. Living near the Seeing Eye Foundation, I decided to run over and let them read it. A Mr. David Loux (manager of Field Operations)

came to the lobby with his dog and greeted me as if he could see me. He heard of the level and made a call to the Foundation. It certainly was real, "even though it never worked out as they had wished." He easily read the Braille, which said, "CARPENTER'S LEVEL." The reason I couldn't read it was because a "sighted person," probably working in the Stanley plant, taped it on upside down.

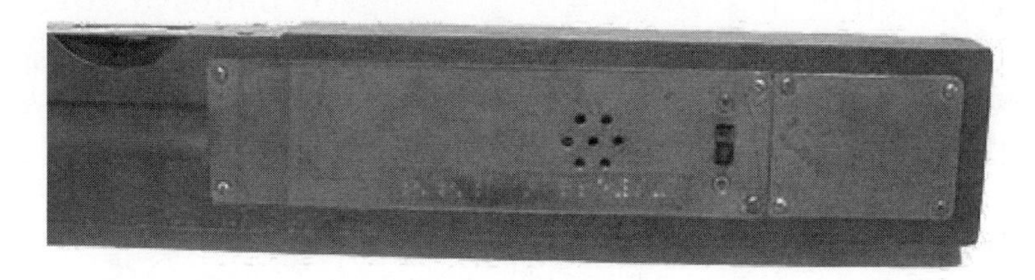

And now the big question, what was a blind person doing with a level? The answer shocked me. Here it is: After the Vietnam War, the U.S. Government decided to help the handicapped Vets by providing classes to put them in gainfully employed situations. They used the word situations, rather than jobs, as in many cases they could never actually hold an industrial job. But they might be able to make a living on their own. Carpentry was one of the classes.

One of the shocks that I received was the equipment that they were trained on, and eventually used: drill press, sander, router, lathe, band saw, and what was the most unbelievable — a table saw, and a jointer! The Rehab Center that I am describing was in Birmingham, Alabama in 1988, but no longer exists.

I could not believe what I was hearing, so I called one of the last remaining blind woodworkers that went to this Rehab Center and got the word directly from the horse's mouth. Mr. Robert West (Washington, GA) filled me in, and provided me with pictures of what he makes — truly great pieces.

Bob told me of the special rules and equipment he uses, and how he goes about using table saws, etc. It's just plain common sense, and it works. Click rules, notch rules, jigs, duplicators, stops, templates, etc. all provide him the safety and accuracy that he needs. His son helps with the assembly, particularly of the large stuff like chest-of-drawers and beds.

He told me one thing that has stuck with me more than anything else. Blind woodworkers have fewer accidents than sighted woodworkers do, because they never lose their concentration!! An interesting and accurate point. Those of us, who have not yet lost a knuckle, should remember it.

Tools have never ceased to amaze me. Here is just one more example of a tool that appeared just when you think you've seen it all.

Author's Note: Although I came to agree that blind people can do woodworking, I never fully understood what any of these shop woodworkers needed with a level. After the article was written, I was surprised to find out that nearby, in Wayne, New Jersey, was a house that had been built predominately by a blind man! In fact a book (*The House the Blind Man Built*, in the Wayne Public Library) and some newspaper articles were written exclusively about this house. Doris and I visited the house and talked to its residents. It is absolutely amazing! I also received a print of Francis A. Burdett and all his tools. Mr Burdett, at age 63 and totally blind, built most of this very nice house. Truth is definitely stranger than fiction.

# 46

## IF YOU CAN'T BEAT 'EM, JOIN 'EM (BUT WATCH OUT) (1999)

For over 25 years Doris and I have been stopping at antique shops and flea markets en route to wherever we were going. As we did a lot of commuting to New England to see our kids, we became very familiar with the shops there — not only the ones on the main thoroughfares but the "backwoods" shops as well.

Now, things are different. I don't have to tell you that finding good tools, or even lousy ones, is tough these days. There were times recently when we came home from a two or three-day trip with so little to show for it that it was embarrassing. I rationalized that tool hunting was not the main purpose of the trip, but that didn't help much.

What really drove me up a tree was that Doris was able to come up with a super piece now and then. Most of the time when we stopped at a shop she didn't bother to go in, and it would turn out that I had wasted my time going in. But when she did get out of the car to go into a shop, I would make a beeline to get in ahead of her because I suspected that there would be a treasure in there somewhere. But this didn't work. The Tool Gods were with her. If she went in, she almost always found something. Not always a real treasure, but a monotony-breaker if nothing else. And it was usually something that I didn't see in my mad rush to upstage her. The frustration of these episodes finally convinced me that, "if you can't beat 'em, join 'em."

So, for the past few years I have been following behind her like a goose and her gosling at every shop she decided to stop at. It has not been at all good for my ego. I have always believed that she has extrasensory perception. How else could she have known whether I won or lost at the Friday night poker games? So, with this as my reasoning, I accepted the situation. If any tool she finds stays in the family, what loss is there? My pride would have to take a back seat. This has worked out "semi-good" over the last few years, but recently things changed a little. No, not a little, a lot! Here's the tale that she has been proudly telling her friends:

We were on our way to see our daughter, and decided to take the long way there across Vermont. We were on one of those backwoods roads. The scenery was pretty and the traffic was light. But I was getting stiff from driving and was looking for a pit stop of one kind or another — hopefully an antique shop. Luck was with me as one loomed up in the distance, and I pulled over. I looked over to see if Doris was going to get out, because I just felt there was something good about this shop. She was out of the car and on her way in without any hesitation. Boy, did I have mixed emotions. I wanted to find something, but at that point the "pickins" had been so slim that it didn't matter to me who found it.

I saw a rack of tools and went straight for them. Doris was wandering around in the wrong section of the shop. Wow, the Tool Gods were going to give me one for a change. But no such luck, I didn't find anything. However, I saw her coming over with a common-looking molding plane in her hand. Well at least she didn't do any better than I did.

Then a funny thing happened. Doris announced that she had bought the plane! (Her idea of buying is taking the piece and letting me pay for it.) But she had never bought any tool without first checking with the "head honcho." I started my usual lecture, which was interrupted by her proclaiming, "I don't care if it cost too much. I want it because it has our name on it, even if it isn't spelled right."

Dead silence from the head honcho. Was it an owner's name or was it the rare "IN-KEEN" stamp? Talk about mixed emotions. "Let me see it," I choked out.

"No, you're not getting this one," was the shocking response.

What was happening here? Was this a full-fledged rebellion, or just a casual independent stand? I'm not going to divulge what I had to promise to get a glimpse of the plane. But it was a truly great piece with a very rare 18th century five-star stamp!

Eighteenth century planes are not really my bag, so I convinced her to let me restore it and sell it. It felt good that I was able to have some say in the matter. But all my good feelings disappeared when I sold HER plane and asked for my cut for restoring it.

"That's your job," she replied, almost puzzled by the request.

"Well how about all the money I put up to pay for it?"

"You always pay for the tools. Why is this one different?"

Once again my good nature had hoisted me on my own petard. Her logic was incomprehensible! I couldn't believe this was happening to me. But let me end this story by telling you that it did.

Some time has passed since that fateful moment, and I can say that I'm over the trauma — or am I?

# 47

## THE BELT AND SUSPENDERS PLANE (2001)

You ask what a belt and suspenders have to do with a plane? Well, it's a philosophy. I'm sure everyone has heard of the man who wanted to be "completely" sure that his pants would stay up. With some people that's a way of life. Now mind you I'm not criticizing. We all have our "ways." But it fits a puzzle that I'm now going to describe.

**The Puzzle:**

As I was readying planes for the CRAFTS auction, I noticed that one of them had a "round-eye" escapement on one side and a "straight-edge" escapement on the other side! See Photos 1 and 2. We're talking about a single-iron chamfer plane, 1³/4" wide with an integral fence and stop in the profile. My first reaction was to put it back in the "non-ready" box, as I felt it was owner-modified. Then I looked closer. It was a crisp, homogeneously patinated John Veit that was almost flawless, and without the slightest sign of modification.

**Photo 1. Chamfer plane. Round-eye escapement left-side opening.**

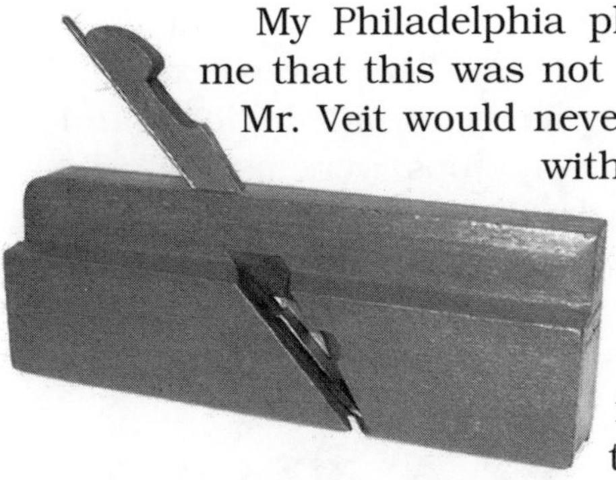

My Philadelphia plane collector friends told me that this was not a manufacturing error, as Mr. Veit would never allow a defect to get out with his name on it. I didn't know how they knew such a thing, but one friend assured me that this was the case. As no one could find any signs of modification, only one conclusion remained: John Veit (who was known for making some pretty specialized tools) experimented with a double escapement. Maybe it was a special order for a user who had trouble with shaving clearance.

**Photo 2. Chamfer plane. Straight-edge escapement right-side opening.**

I put the plane away for another day. Hopefully, I would get further information. But then the bigger question struck me. Why did some planes have a round-eye escapement (completely through the body) and others a straight-edge escapement (open only on one side of the body)? OK, so it's not a life and death problem, but it does require an insight that is a cut above the average tool question.

Next were the phone calls to friends who had knowledge of the geometry of planes. Although no one had a firm answer, there were threads of logic wafting through. Many of the answers stated meaningful variables such as thickness of shaving, type of wood, pitch of blade, type of cut, etc., but none could explain all the exceptions that I found. An unfailing reason had to be found. (In other words: the thing was bugging me.)

**The Search:**

One of the best ways to solve problems is to look at the data effecting the problem. My friends and I looked at all our wooden planes and sorted out almost all of the variables.

There were a few exceptions, some explainable, and a very small number (mostly homemade planes) were not. Here's a condensation of the thousand or so side-escapement planes that we looked at:

1) Almost every molding plane had a straight opening only on the right side of the plane. There were explainable exceptions, such as completely profiled "left-handed" planes. Integral fences and/or stops were part of almost every profile, and therefore the blade did not extend beyond both sides of the body. See Photo 3.

**Photo 3. Top: Left-handed molding plane with left-side straight escapement. Bottom: Standard right-handed molding plane with right-side straight escapement.**

2) Most of the rabbet planes and all of the dado planes had skewed blades with a leading right edge. Both had round openings completely through the body. Most openings were tapered to be larger on the left side, to match the skew of the blade. See Photo 4. Some rabbet blades were not skewed (e.g. coach rabbets) and as such the opening was not tapered.

An exception was a wide square-blade rabbet that had the opening tapered from the centerline of the plane body outward in both directions. See Photo 5. As integral fences and stops were not part of the profile on either rabbets or dados, the blade extended slightly beyond the body on both sides to allow it to sink the cut without interference from the body. In machine shop parlance this is called plunging.

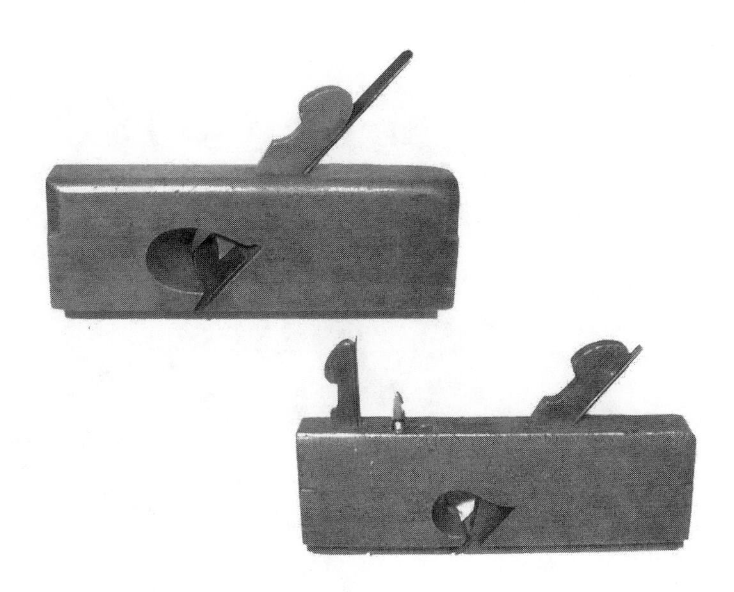

**Photo 4. Top: Skewed rabbet plane with left-side round tapered escapement. Bottom: Skewed dado plane with left-side round tapered escapement.**

3) The sash filletsters, sometimes called "back filletsters" because they cut on the far (or back) side of the work, were of two styles. Both styles had straight openings, and both had fences attached to arms. One style (Photo 6, mostly Philadelphia makers) opened on the right side, and the second style (Photo 7, mostly English makers) opened on the left side. However, as sash filletsters cut the putty rabbet that seats the glass (which is not very deep), the full width of the blade rarely, if ever, came into play.

Both styles had skewed blades: the right-side opening planes had the left-leading tip of the blade into the shoulder, and the left-side opening planes had the right-trailing corner of the blade into the shoulder. Most all the skewed planes that I checked (of

**Photo 5. Square-blade rabbet plane with double tapered round escapement.**

**Photo 6. Sash filletster, Philadelphia style with right-side straight escapement.**

all types), had the tip of the blade into the shoulder. It tended to hold the plane into the cut better, and it also acted as a nicker, when an individual nicker was not present. However the sash filletster (mentioned above) with the trailing edge into the shoulder worked very well for me. Probably because the fence on the opposite side locked it into the cut, and there was a nicker present.

4) The moving filletsters, sometimes called "fore filletsters" because they cut on the near (or fore) side of the work, were also of two styles: fenced without arms (the more common type) and fenced with arms (much rarer). Here is where the cheese really started to bind. The ones without arms and with an underslung fence sliding on screws that were in the sole, all had straight openings on the right side. The fence hid a portion of the blade no matter where it was positioned.

**Photo 7. Sash filletster, English style with left-side straight escapement.**

See Photo 8. A rare model with short arms, which also disallowed the fence to uncover the blade fully, had the straight opening on the right side too. BUT, the second style, with the fence on full-length arms, had a round opening on the left side! See Photo 9. Both styles had skewed blades with the right edge leading into the shoulder.

5) There was a combined sash & moving filletster that had its fence on full-length arms. It was boxed on both sides, had nickers and depth stops on both sides, and had the round opening on the left. It also had a skewed blade with the right edge leading. However, as it cut from either side, sometimes the leading edge went into the shoulder, while other times the trailing edge did the same on the opposite side. But the trailing-edge side was used only when the plane was cutting as a sash filletster (with the fence opposite and a nicker in play on that side). As previously stated, that configuration worked fine.

**Photo 8. Moving filletster, without arms with right-side straight escapement.**

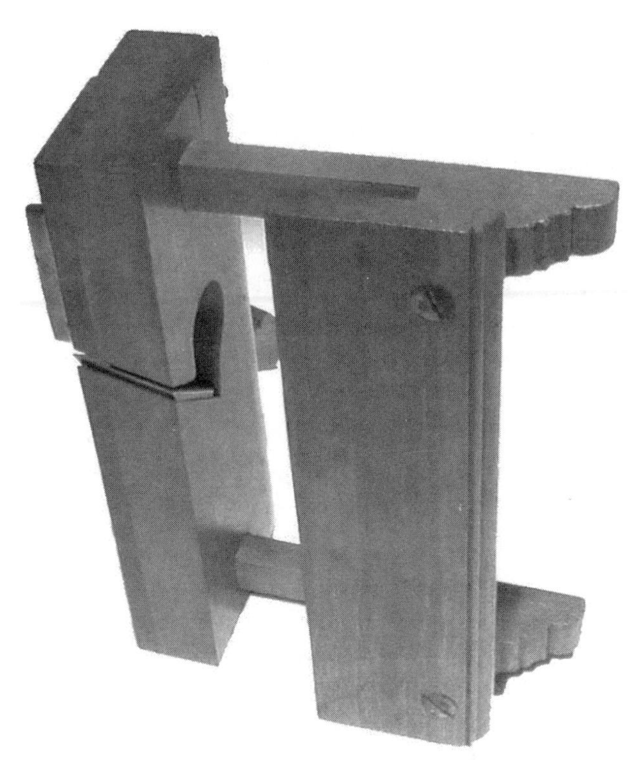

**Photo 9. Moving filletster, with arms with left-side round escapement.**

**The Analysis:**

So much for the data. It had me more confused than when I started. . . . Now what?

In desperation, I asked my wife Doris! Don't laugh. When I worked in aero-space, I solved a few problems by putting them to people completely unaware of the facts. I'll never forget how the stress-crack fiasco in the wings of the Concorde was solved many years ago: in a men's room discussion between two engineers that was interrupted by a machinist who knew nothing about aerodynamics. Doris had helped solve similar problems by pointing me in the direction that I wasn't able to "see." In this case it was embarrassingly simple: "Use all the planes, and see what happens differently."

When it came time to use the moving filletster with the full-length arms, I saw that the fence was previously set about an inch away from the body. . . . The light bulb went on! . . . If I wanted to cut a rabbet that was wider than the width of the blade, I would have to take two (or more) passes. The first pass would be at full-blade width against the final shoulder of the rabbet. See Sketch 1. I thought about "nibbling" shorter widths from the near edge, but the fence

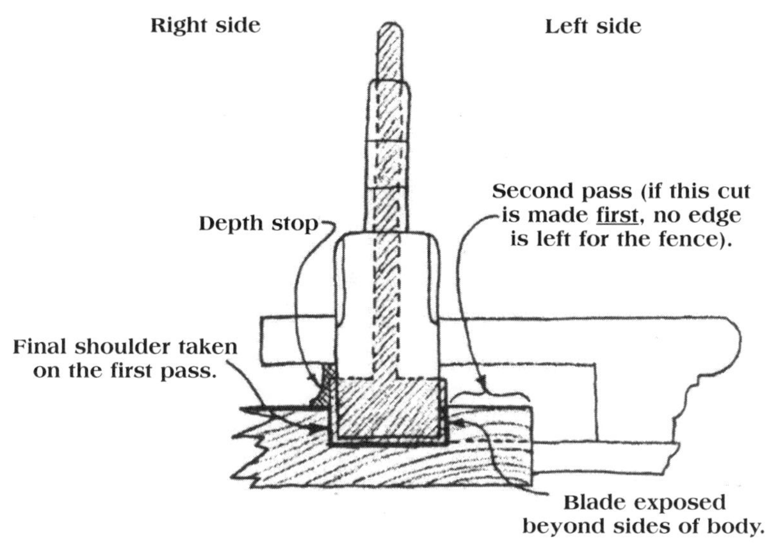


**Sketch 1. Moving filletster with arms. Front view — left side opening.**

was so thin (under 1/2") that it wouldn't catch the edge on the second pass. Later models did increase the thickness of the fence to allow nibbling, but kept the round opening to give the user the option of full-cut or nibble. The plane could also be used (in either manner) to clean up a wide rabbet that was originally roughed out with a saw. The key was that the blade was exposed beyond the sides of the body just like a dado or rabbet!

There it was: those planes that plunged at the full-blade width (with both edges of the blade exposed beyond the body) required a round opening to help curl, direct and clear the shaving.

One fact which helped support the theory above was the opening in the skates of plow planes. Of the 100 or so that were looked at, all had the circular opening in the skate - because the blade always plunged at full width. Whoa! All but one. It was a V-cut plow (some models were called shiphawk planes). Why did this lone exception have a straight opening? Because it never cut the full width of the blade. The depth stop would not allow it to do so! That seemed to clinch the premise.

Another interesting fact was that all sash filletsters had flat, skewed blades exposed on both sides, similar to the moving filletster. *But* they cut up against a shoulder on one side with most of the other side of the blade free of the cut. Therefore they weren't cutting at full-width, and didn't need the eye. See Sketch 2.

You might ask, "Didn't rabbet planes cut like that most of the time?" Yes, but not when the full profile of the rabbet was wider than the blade (e.g. when cleaning up a wide rabbet joint.) See Sketch 3.

"How about dados? They cut against shoulders." See Sketch 4. Dados, like plows, needed the eye badly, as the full-blade-width shaving was "locked" between the sides of the groove and needed help getting out. Plus, dados cut cross-grain, which we know is a tougher direction to get a good curl.

Speaking of cross-grain — the skewed blade on the sash filletster might seem like a waste, as it only cut along the

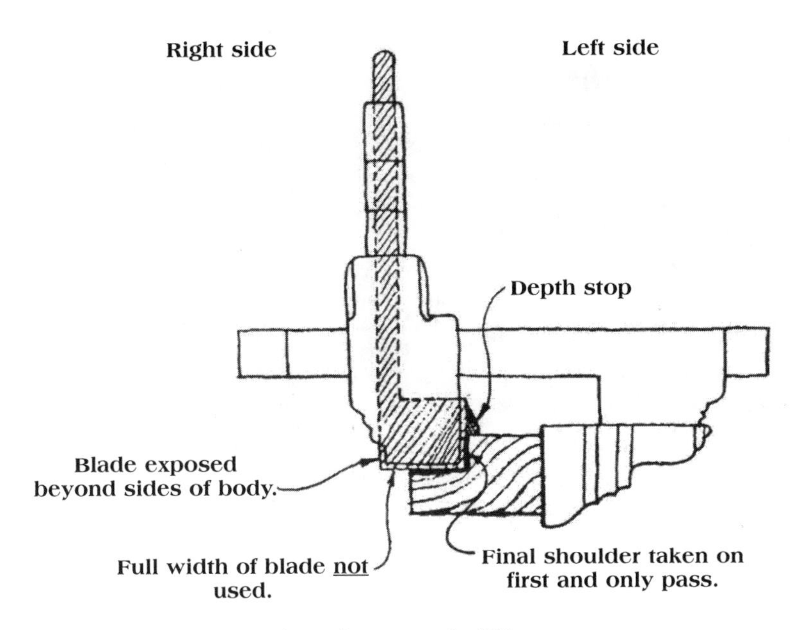


**Sketch 2. Sash filletster**
**Front view — left side opening (English style).**

grain. Another Belt and Suspenders? No! A skewed blade helped to curl a flat-cut shaving. The best example is a spill plane. It had an exaggerated skew that produced a curl that was so tight that it ended up looking like a hollow rod. So, both styles of the sash filletsters had their blades skewed to gain this advantage.

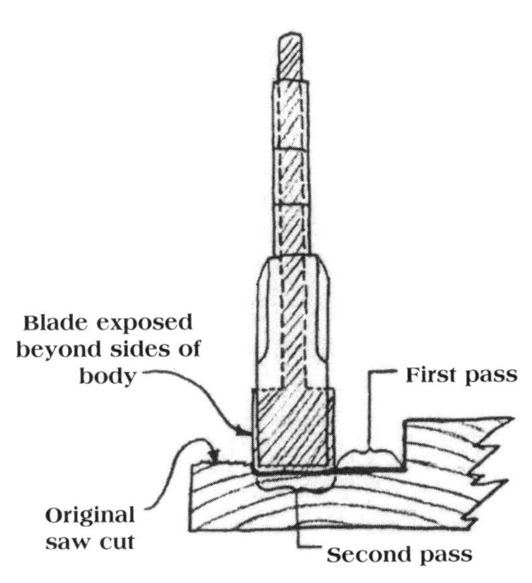


**Sketch 3. Rabbet Plane, Front View**

A somewhat obvious question is, "If the round opening was so effective in clearing out the shaving, why didn't they make all planes with a round-eye?"

That one is easy. It cost more. Some manufacturers offered the roundeye at an additional price, but the old timers used the slogan that our industrial engineers use today: GOOD ENOUGH IS BEST. If they didn't need it, they were not going to pay for it. Maybe they should have paid for it, as witnessed by the many botch jobs created by users who tried to open the straight throats for better clearance.

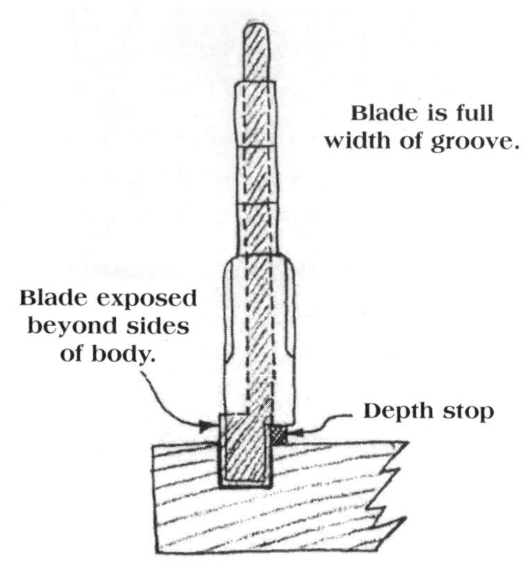


**Sketch 4. Dado Plane, Front View**

**The Summary:**

Planemaking was a lot more complex than many of us realize. In most cases things were done for good reasons. It may be difficult for us to grasp those reasons today, because of the many subtleties and economic differences involved. But if you look hard enough, at enough examples, you will probably find an answer. And the answer often shows that most craftsmen of yesteryear got things done by the "what-works" method more than the academic approach.

John Veit might have had a workable idea with his "double" escapement plane. (It will still bug me until I know what he had in mind). However, based upon the rarity of this plane, I would have to conclude that the idea just wasn't worth the effort. But the "Belt and Suspender Plane" stands as a monument to the way things were accomplished by those men of yesteryear. And, it prodded me into digging into the puzzle of the round escapement versus the straight escapement.

# 48

## AN ALL-WOOD STANLEY NO. 1 (REALLY!) (2001)

Three years ago, *Chip Chats,* the magazine for the National Wood Carvers Association, published an article about a "hand-carved wooden plane." It was a Stanley No.4 with most of the plane carved from wood, but all the hardware and blades were the original iron, brass and steel. As far as I was concerned it was about the same as what a patternmaker would do. I decided to try to do one completely out of wood! Yes, completely — every screw, nut, washer, stud, pin, rivet, casting, blade, and even the spring in the cap. And to make it more of a challenge, I decided on the smallest of the Stanley bench planes, the Number One. See Photo 1.

If it were to qualify as a carving, and not a pattern, each of the individual parts that were originally cast in one piece had to be carved in one piece. So, the body, which a patternmaker would have glued-up out of eight different pieces, was hogged out of one piece of butternut. (Butternut is the choice over basswood, when you want some grain to show.) The frog and the cap were also butternut. The smaller more intricate pieces were made from boxwood. Almost any species of boxwood works fine for the parts that are not threaded. But when you are trying to make a tiny 8-32 screw from wood, you're best sticking to Turkish boxwood.

**Photo 1**

The knob and handle were carved from Brazilian rosewood. See Photo 2.

I quickly learned that to make the plane "work" the tolerances had to be almost as close as the real ones. In a few

**Photo 2**

cases they were as tight as plus or minus .002"! The rest of the time they wandered up to plus or minus .010" (about twice the thickness of your hair). If it were to be a real challenge, the tough internal portions of the body casting had to be done as a true carving: *no router.* I roughed out two body castings, as I felt I'd screw up the first one somewhere. I got tremendous confidence when the first one came out clean, with no glue-ups or wood fills. In fact, there are no glue-ups or fills anywhere on the plane.

As I made this plane over three years ago, and it was written-up in the August 1998 *Fine Woodworking* magazine, I have been asked many times to make a production run for resale. Some even granted me the O.K. to piece-up the body as a patternmaker would. I've given it some thought, but it's just too much work for an old retired guy. I didn't keep time records, but my best estimate is around 25 hours, including the design and setup. A younger, better carver could beat the heck out of this in production.

What turned out to be the toughest job was the threading. When I used a die for the male pieces, the diameter had to be precisely matched to the die. It was not like working in metal where the die brings it to size no matter where the diameter starts. I ruined quite a few wooden threaded pieces before I swung over to "chasing" them on a lathe. (If you are interested, see my book *Restoring Antique Tools* for the details of this technique.) Some of the screws still had to be made with a die, and many had to be done over.

Tapping wasn't as hard, particularly if it were done into flat grain rather than end grain. Where needed (especially in the butternut), boxwood threaded inserts were made. I didn't think I could get away with wood for the flat spring under the cap, as it was only 1/32" thick. But after three years, this wooden spring has held, and still maintains good pressure. I gave the rivet that holds the spring to the cap a light head before driving it, very much like the iron one in the real piece. The blade was not stamped STANLEY for obvious reasons, even though I didn't think the Stanley Company would have minded.

It surprised me to find that wood could do almost everything that metal could do. Not with as much wearability, or strength naturally, but with pretty decent mimicry. The blade actually cut a tiny shaving from the corner of a pine board! And I am proud to say that every part works exactly like its iron cousin, and matches it dimensionally. A true reproduction carving.

**"Ivory miniature tools? No way! I'm a save the elephant person."**

**"No problem, these are made from old piano keys."**

# 49

## MIXED EMOTIONS
## (2002)

Back in the '70s (almost sounds like ancient history), there was a very quaint antique shop near the village of Hubbardton, Vermont that was run by one of the original antique toolers. The shop was called Iron Horse Antiques, and the dealer was Vernon Ward. He put out a catalog that was one of the few places where you could see hundreds of antique tools at the same time. To a relative beginner, the Iron Horse was spectacular.

As part of our New England "wanderings," Doris and I decided to stay on Lake Bomoseen (just next to Hubbardton) for a nice quiet vacation. Fishing, antiquing, eating-out and just plain relaxing; it had it all. I neglected to mention to her that it was only a brisk walk from the Iron Horse.

It's not hard to figure out that the eating-out and the relaxing parts were overshadowed by the fishing and the antiquing. Yep, most days I was up early and out on the lake until the shop opened later in the day. Then browsing amongst what I considered the best collection of tools anywhere. It was high living.

The last day of the vacation, I promised Doris that I would be home early, so she could go shopping for gifts before we left. I really had every intention of doing just that. However, fate stepped in. Vern was going to Rutland that morning and had no time for me, except to tell me that a small dealer had called with a great piece, but needed the money quickly. Vern benevolently turned it over to me, as the dealer lived nearby. Wow! A chance to get a good piece at a wholesale price.

It was a beautiful house right on the lake with a garage full of antiques. The daughter was getting married that weekend and some of the costs were getting out of line. Some extra bucks would help. OK, I had some extra bucks, and couldn't wait to see the piece.

It was the gunmetal Millers Patent. It took my breath away. It's the same one that still hangs on my wall, and has been on the cover of the *American Woodworker* Tool Calender and the CRAFTS *Tool Shed Treasury*. I never even knew that they made tools like that. The downside was that the dealer had a fair idea of its value and asked a price that also took my breath away. (I bought my first car for less.) After much agonizing, I turned him down, and went back to our cottage feeling very low.

"Where have you been for so long, and what's with the long face?" was what greeted me. I just said that I had an opportunity to buy a great tool, but if I did I would have no money left for her to buy gifts. I don't think she believed that was the real reason, but it was fine with her and off to town we went. (She didn't spend much, as she has always been a rather frugal person.)

We packed, said our goodbyes and headed south for home. I was unusually quiet for the first 50 miles. Finally, she asked me to "spill it." I let it all out: the beauty of the plane, the fact that I never bought anything expensive, all the trips that I took her on, all the restaurants that I took her to, and on and on. She finally cut it off and asked the price. I lied a little.

"Do you have enough money?" she asked.

"Just."

A smile and a hug and I pulled into the nearest phone booth. Yes, the plane was still for sale, and yes he would drop the price a little. But he needed the money that day, and if I came there within the next hour or so, it could be mine.

Going the extra 100 miles was a little much, and I thought that would be the "straw." But no, Doris was all for turning back. I was super delighted, and if I knew how to do one of those TV spin-turns I would have done one.

The transaction was quick and pleasant, and we wished them a happy wedding. I couldn't get out of there fast enough. After a few miles I pulled over and just stared at the piece. Doris took it away from me as she was afraid I would keep looking at it rather than the road. It was a grand day.

After about 15 minutes, a strange feeling started to creep over me. I wasn't feeling very well either. I stopped the car, got out and breathed deeply to get my color back. Was it something I ate? Not likely. I really knew what it was, but was too ashamed to admit it. However, it didn't take Doris very long to figure it out.

"Mr. Conservative has finally jumped into the deep water," was her analysis. With a few rational and consoling remarks, she had me back to normal, and we were on our way.

Needless to say, the particular piece was well worth the money. It was one of the best investments that I made in my early collecting days. But I will never forget the wildly mixed emotions of that day.

# 50

## THE WAY IT WAS
## (2001)

Old collectors will get a kick out of this stroll down memory lane. New collectors will shake their heads and roll their eyes, and (I hope), give out a chuckle or two. Yes, tool collecting has changed, but so has everything else in life. This article is more about the change in the people who collect tools, namely Doris and me. I'm sure that there are others like us. Let's go back a few years (more like 25). Put your time-machine cap on and try to imagine the days when there was no horn blowing if you had a millisecond delay at a traffic light. Picture us in our Chevy wagon on our way up to the "wilds" of New England to get the third most important thing in life. (My slogan was different than the Marines. It was: FAMILY, COUNTRY, and TOOLS.)

In those days, it was very effective to have a string of "pickers." As pickers are practically extinct today, some of the new collectors might not recognize the term. A picker was a semi-knowledgeable person who went to all the small country auctions, where all kinds of treasures could be gleaned at a mere pittance. If you had a good relationship with the picker, he would save all this stuff until you came by, and then unload it all in one lot. A "good relationship" meant that you didn't whine about some of his stupid purchases, but merely plunked down the money that he asked for without a lot of hesitation. This was not as painful as it might sound. His price was always twice what he paid for the lot, and usually one or two good pieces covered it. At the first opportunity, you just trashed the meaningless stuff, rather than take up precious space in the car. It seems unbelievable today, but we came back from those trips with the car bottoming on the springs and the back window completely blocked.

Our travel program was a lot different then. We never made reservations, because we never knew how long we were going to be at each picker. We didn't start looking for a motel until after dinner, when there weren't many really nice places left. Expensive places to stay (or eat) were pretty much out of the program. That never bothered me, but as I look back now, I realize it must not have been too exciting for Doris. But she was a real trooper about it (at least for the first few years).

One trip still stands out in my mind. It was in the dead of winter, and we just about got into a motel in White River Junction, Vermont. The snow was starting to come down, but the roads were reasonably clear at the time. I had not seen the last picker on the schedule for the day, so right after supper I gave him a call. Yep, he would be home that evening. Doris would have no part of driving in a snowstorm to see someone who MIGHT have a worthwhile tool or two.

So, off I went by myself, to finalize the day. I felt good about the pickins that day, as the back of the wagon was almost filled. I sing a lot (not very well), and I was at the top of my voice as I moved along through that blinding snow. Without the least warning, my rear window exploded! And I mean exploded. I was sure it was some lunatic with a shotgun, so I sped away. Only when I was "safe" did I pull over to assess the damages. There was nothing left of the window, but oddly enough there was very little glass inside the wagon. A shotgun blast would have certainly put a ton of glass inside. The contact must have heated up and the below-zero temperature did the rest. (Only later did I learn that General Motors was having trouble with the contact of the rear defroster with the hatchback window.) I journeyed on to my destination, without much spirit, as I could picture the problem getting home. The picker and I taped cardboard to the window. It helped, but I was concerned that someone could easily help himself to my precious cargo when I parked at the motel. Doris said that no one in his right mind would steal "that junk." But I lugged most of it upstairs to our room anyway. You can imagine what that small room looked like with boxes of stuff everywhere.

The next day I had a sheet of plastic temporarily installed in the window. (GM replaced it properly later). We had one more day of stops. Although Doris was ready to call it quits, I convinced her to bundle up, as the plastic didn't fit too well and the heater was struggling to keep the icicles off our noses. Naturally, I had to tell each person, wherever we stopped, the story of the exploding window. Maybe they felt sorry for me, or maybe it was my lucky day, as I had one of my better tooling days.

We bounded in and out of the car in those days, not wanting to waste a moment. Today, it's a project just getting out of the car. And I have to have someone carry the boxes if they are too heavy. The only saving grace is that I no longer buy bulky iron, and getting boxes of stuff really does not happen that often. Today we call ahead for reservations, both for the motel and for dinner. We stay at some very nice places and eat at some excellent restaurants. But all the pickers are gone, and very few shops handle tools anymore. It's just not the same. But I'll never forget THE WAY IT WAS.

**"Doris, you won't believe what happened!"**

## THE END

As I went over each story for corrections or updating, I relived the past 28 years. I never realized how antique tools became such a strong part of my marriage and my life. These tools, and the fellowship they brought, amounted to a third of my lifetime. Pretty awesome, as my grandson would say.

With any hobby, there are things that eventually become tiring. But with antique tools there are so many "side roads" of activity that a new project always replaces one that is getting stale. The stories in this book reflect the variety of things to do, places to go, and people to see, while collecting.

I got a warm feeling about all these stories as I put *Tool Tales* together. I hope you did too.